Cambridge First Certificate in English 2

WITH ANSWERS

Official examination papers from University of Cambridge ESOL Examinations

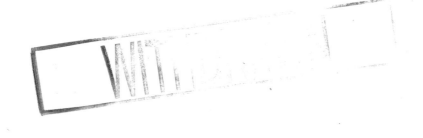

CAMBRIDGE
UNIVERSITY PRESS

CAMBRIDGE UNIVERSITY PRESS
Cambridge, New York, Melbourne, Madrid, Cape Town, Singapore,
São Paulo, Delhi, Dubai, Tokyo

Cambridge University Press
The Edinburgh Building, Cambridge CB2 8RU, UK

www.cambridge.org
Information on this title: www.cambridge.org/9780521714549

© Cambridge University Press 2008

First published 2008
3rd printing 2009

Printed in the United Kingdom at the University Press, Cambridge

A catalogue record for this publication is available from the British Library

ISBN 978-0-521-714549 Student's Book with answers
ISBN 978-0-521-714532 Student's Book without answers
ISBN 978-0-521-714563 Audio CDs (2)
ISBN 978-0-521-714556 Self-study Pack (Student's Book with answers and Audio CDs (2))

Cambridge University Press has no responsibility for the persistence or
accuracy of URLs for external or third-party internet websites referred to in
this publication, and does not guarantee that any content on such websites is,
or will remain, accurate or appropriate. Information regarding prices, travel
timetables and other factual information given in this work are correct at
the time of first printing but Cambridge University Press does not guarantee
the accuracy of such information thereafter.

Contents

Thanks and acknowledgements

The authors and publishers acknowledge the following sources of copyright material and are grateful for the permissions granted. While every effort has been made, it has not always been possible to identify the sources of all the material used, or to trace all copyright holders. If any omissions are brought to our notice, we will be happy to include the appropriate acknowledgements on reprinting.

For the texts on p. 8 and on p. 30, from *Cross my Heart and Hope to Die* by Sheila Radley, 1992. By permission of Constable and Robinson Publishing Ltd; for the text on p. 10, 'The Netball Captain' by Suzie Ellis, from Hello! Online www.hello-online.ru. Copyright © 2003 National Association of Teachers of English; for the article on p. 13, 'Style Merchants' by Jo Foley, *Illustrated London News*, 1998; for the text on p. 32, 'Living in the Valley' by Mike Bell from *Peak and Pennine*, March 1998, © Mike Bell; for the adapted texts by Nina Hathway on p. 35, 'Confident people. What's their secret?' *Woman's Weekly*, February 1997, and on p. 79 from 'Theme Park', *Woman's Weekly*, July 1996, © Copyright IPC Media Ltd, all rights reserved; for the articles from the *Independent* on p. 52, 'The Shell Artist' by Peter Cooke, 27 April 1996, and on p. 74, 'The Film Critic' by Mark Adams, 11 October 1996, © Independent News and Media Limited; for the adapted article on p. 54, 'Chips with Everything' from *Caterer and Hotel Keeper*, 29 January 1998, © The Caterer Group; for the adapted text on p. 63, 'Secret London' by Andrew Duncan, New Holland Publishers (UK Limited); for the adapted article on p. 76, 'Fun at the Dentist's?' by Rose Rouse, *Guardian*, 31 December 1996, © Rose Rouse; for the adapted text on p. 84, 'Downhill Racer' by David Allsopp, *Midweek*, 2–6 February, 1995; for the article on p. 85, 'See you in three years says jogger on lap of the world' by Russell Jenkins, *The Times*, 7 December 1996, © N I Syndication Limited.

For permission to reproduce copyright photographs:

Art Directors & TRIP/C Kapolka for p. 32; The Merrion Hotel, Dublin for p. 54; W Lloyd Jerome for p. 77; Steve Bloom Images/Alamy for p. 90.

Colour section

Alamy/Harold R Stinnette Photo Stock pC6 (bl), Alamy/Mixa Co Ltd pC8 (b), Alamy/Photostock Files pC6 (tr); **Art Directors & Trip** pC1 (b), Art Directors & Trip pC16 (t), Art Directors & Trip/B Gadsby pC13 (b), Art Directors & Trip/Helene Rogers pC6 (tl), Art Directors & Trip/J Stanley pC13 (t); **Corbis**/Jason Hosling/Zefa pC14 (b); **Getty Images**/ Howard Kingsnorth pC9 (t), Getty Images/Alan Klehr pC8 (t), Getty Images/Andy Caulfield pC9 (b), Getty Images/Chris Ladd pC14 (t), Getty Images/Daniel Pangbourne pC14 (c), Getty Images/John Warden pC7 (cr), Getty Images/Stewart Cohen pC5 (tr), Getty/Don Johnston pC7 (tr); **John Birdsall** pC5 (b), pC12 (b), pC15 (bl); **Life File**/Angela Maynard pC15 (br); **Pictures Colour Library** pC4 (all), pC7 (b); **Robert Harding**/Dr Müller pC12 (t); **Sally & Richard Greenhill** pC1 (t), pC16 (b), Sally & Richard Greenhill/Richard Greenhill pC6 (br); **Shout Pictures**/John Callan pC15 (tl); **VCL**/Alistair Berry pC15 (tr).

Artwork by Oxford Designers & Illustrators

Picture research by Alison Prior

Design concept by Peter Ducker

Cover design by David Lawson

The recordings which accompany this book were made at Studio AVP, London.

Introduction

This collection of four complete practice tests comprises papers from the University of Cambridge ESOL Examinations First Certificate in English (FCE) examination; students can practise these tests on their own or with the help of a teacher.

The FCE examination is part of a suite of general English examinations produced by Cambridge ESOL. This suite consists of five examinations that have similar characteristics but are designed for different levels of English language ability. Within the five levels, FCE is at Level B2 in the Council of Europe's *Common European Framework of Reference for Languages: Learning, teaching, assessment*. It has also been accredited by the Qualifications and Curriculum Authority in the UK as a Level 1 ESOL certificate in the National Qualifications Framework. The FCE examination is widely recognised in commerce and industry and in individual university faculties and other educational institutions.

Examination	Council of Europe Framework Level	UK National Qualifications Framework Level
CPE Certificate of Proficiency in English	C2	3
CAE Certificate in Advanced English	C1	2
FCE First Certificate in English	B2	1
PET Preliminary English Test	B1	Entry 3
KET Key English Test	A2	Entry 2

Further information

The information contained in this practice book is designed to be an overview of the exam. For a full description of all of the above exams including information about task types, testing focus and preparation, please see the relevant handbooks which can be obtained from Cambridge ESOL at the address below or from the website at: www.CambridgeESOL.org

University of Cambridge ESOL Examinations
1 Hills Road
Cambridge CB1 2EU
United Kingdom

Telephone: +44 1223 553997
Fax: +44 1223 553621
e-mail: ESOLHelpdesk@ucles.org.uk

The structure of FCE: an overview

The FCE examination consists of five papers.

Paper 1   Reading   1 hour
This paper consists of **three parts**, each containing a text and some questions. Part 3 may contain two or more shorter related texts. There are **30 questions** in total, including multiple-choice, gapped text and multiple-matching questions.

Paper 2   Writing   1 hour 20 minutes
This paper consists of **two parts** which carry equal marks. In Part 1, which is **compulsory**, candidates have to write either a letter or an email of between 120 and 150 words. In Part 2, there are four tasks from which candidates **choose one** to write about. The range of tasks from which questions may be drawn includes an article, an essay, a letter, a report, a review and a short story. The last question is based on the set books. These books remain on the list for two years. Look on the website, or contact the Cambridge ESOL Local Secretary in your area for the up-to-date list of set books. The question on the set books has two options from which candidates **choose one** to write about. In this part, candidates have to write between 120 and 180 words.

Paper 3   Use of English   45 minutes
This paper consists of **four parts** and tests control of English grammar and vocabulary. There are **42 questions** in total. The tasks include gap-filling exercises, word formation and sentence transformation.

Paper 4   Listening   40 minutes (approximately)
This paper consists of **four parts**. Each part contains a recorded text or texts and some questions, including multiple-choice, sentence completion, and multiple-matching. Each text is heard twice. There is a total of **30 questions**.

Paper 5   Speaking   14 minutes
This paper consists of **four parts**. The standard test format is two candidates and two examiners. One examiner takes part in the conversation while the other examiner listens. Both examiners give marks. Candidates will be given photographs and other visual and written material to look at and talk about. Sometimes candidates will talk with the other candidates, sometimes with the examiner and sometimes with both.

Grading

The overall FCE grade is based on the total score gained in all five papers. Each paper is weighted to 40 marks. Therefore, the five FCE papers total 200 marks, after weighting. It is not necessary to achieve a satisfactory level in all five papers in order to pass the examination. Certificates are given to candidates who pass the examination with grade A, B or C. A is the highest. D and E are failing grades. All candidates are sent a Statement of Results which includes a graphical profile of their performance in each paper and shows their relative performance in each one.

   For further information on grading and results, go to the website (see page 5).

Test 1

PAPER 1   READING (1 hour)

Part 1

You are going to read an extract from a novel. For questions **1–8**, choose the answer (**A, B, C** or **D**) which you think fits best according to the text.

Mark your answers **on the separate answer sheet**.

Many trees in the Brackham area were brought down in the terrible storms that March. The town itself lost two great lime trees from the former market square. The disappearance of such prominent features had altered the appearance of the town centre entirely, to the annoyance of its more conservative inhabitants.

Among the annoyed, under more normal circumstances, would have been Chief Inspector Douglas Pelham, head of the local police force. But at the height of that week's storm, when the wind brought down even the mature walnut tree in his garden, Pelham had in fact been in no fit state to notice. A large and healthy man, he had for the first time in his life been seriously ill with an attack of bronchitis.

When he first complained of an aching head and tightness in his chest, his wife, Molly, had tried to persuade him to go to the doctor. Convinced that the police force could not do without him, he had, as usual, ignored her and attempted to carry on working. Predictably, though he wouldn't have listened to anyone who tried to tell him so, this had the effect of fogging his memory and shortening his temper.

line 16 It was only when his colleague, Sergeant Lloyd, took the initiative and drove him to the doctor's door that he finally gave in. By that time, he didn't have the strength left to argue with her. In no time at all, she was taking him along to the chemist's to get his prescribed antibiotics and then home to his unsurprised wife who sent him straight to bed.

When Molly told him, on the Thursday morning, that the walnut tree had been brought down during the night, Pelham hadn't been able to take it in. On Thursday evening, he had asked weakly about damage to the house, groaned thankfully when he heard there was none, and pulled the sheets over his head.

It wasn't until Saturday, when the antibiotics took effect, his temperature dropped and he got up, that he realised with a shock that the loss of the walnut tree had made a permanent difference to the appearance of the living-room. The Pelhams' large house stood in a sizeable garden. It had not come cheap, but even so Pelham had no regrets about buying it. The leafy garden had created an impression of privacy. Now, though, the storm had changed his outlook.

Previously, the view from the living-room had featured the handsome walnut tree. This had not darkened the room because there was also a window on the opposite wall, but it had provided interesting patterns of light and shade that disguised the true state of the worn furniture that the family had brought with them from their previous house.

line 33 With the tree gone, the room seemed cruelly bright, its worn furnishings exposed in all their shabbiness. And the view from the window didn't bear looking at. The tall house next door, previously hidden by the tree, was now there, dominating the outlook with its unattractive purple bricks and external pipes. It seemed to have a great many upstairs windows, all of them watching the Pelhams' every movement.

'Doesn't it look terrible?' Pelham croaked to his wife.

But Molly, standing in the doorway, sounded more pleased than dismayed. 'That's what I've been telling you ever since we came here. We have to buy a new sofa, whatever it costs.'

1 Why were some people in Brackham annoyed after the storm?

   A The town looked different.
   B The police had done little to help.
   C No market could be held.
   D Fallen trees had not been removed.

2 In the third paragraph, what do we learn about Chief Inspector Pelham's general attitude to his work?

   A He finds it extremely annoying.
   B He is sure that he fulfils a vital role.
   C He considers the systems are not clear enough.
   D He does not trust the decisions made by his superiors.

3 Who does 'her' in line 16 refer to?

   A Molly Pelham
   B the doctor
   C the chemist
   D Sergeant Lloyd

4 When Inspector Pelham's wife first told him about the walnut tree, he appeared to be

   A worried.
   B shocked.
   C saddened.
   D uninterested.

5 What aspect of the Pelhams' furniture does 'shabbiness' in line 33 describe?

   A its colour
   B its condition
   C its position
   D its design

6 As a result of the storm, the Pelhams' living-room

   A was pleasantly lighter.
   B felt less private.
   C had a better view.
   D was in need of repair.

7 Why did Molly sound pleased by her husband's comment?

   A It proved that he was well again.
   B She agreed about the tree.
   C She thought he meant the sofa.
   D It was what she expected him to say.

8 From what we learn of Inspector Pelham, he could best be described as

   A open-minded.
   B well-liked.
   C warm-hearted.
   D strong-willed.

Part 2

You are going to read a magazine interview with a sportswoman. Seven sentences have been removed from the article. Choose from the sentences **A–H** the one which fits each gap (**9–15**). There is one extra sentence which you do not need to use.

Mark your answers **on the separate answer sheet**.

The Netball Captain

In our series on women in sport, Suzie Ellis went to meet England's netball captain.

Kendra Slawinski is captain of England's netball team. When I met her, she'd had a typical day for the weeks leading up to next month's World Championships: a day's teaching at a local school followed by a training session in the local supermarket car park.

I was surprised to hear about her training venue.

'Don't you get strange looks?' I asked her. 'I'm too involved in what I'm doing – concentrating on my movements and my feet – to see anything else,' she said. 'I might notice cars slow down out of the corner of my eye, but that's all.'

'My whole life now is all about making sure I'm at my absolute best for the Championships,' says Kendra. ' **9** ' These are her fourth World Championships and they are guaranteed to be the biggest ever, with 27 nations taking part.

'We'll have home support behind us, which is so special,' she says. 'And it's important that the reputation of netball in this country should be improved. **10** A home crowd will have expectations and give more support. People will expect us to start the tournament with a good game.'

Their first game is against Barbados and it comes immediately after the opening ceremony. ' **11** They have lots of ability.'

The England team are currently ranked fourth in the world. But, as Kendra points out, the World Championships will be tough. 'You have to push yourself to play each day, there's no rest between games as in a series. And you can still win an international series if you lose the first game. **12** '

In the fifteen years since she has been playing at top level, the sport has become harder, faster. On court, players are more aggressive. 'You don't do all that training not to come out a winner,' says Kendra.

' **13** We're all friendlier after the game.'

Netball is also taking a far more scientific approach to fitness testing.

'It is essential that we all think and train like world-class players,' says Kendra.

' **14** I see my role as supporting and encouraging the rest of the team.'

'From the very beginning, my netball career has always been carefully planned,' she says. ' **15** '

Doubtless she will coach young players in the future, but at the moment her eyes are firmly set on her last big event. As she leads out her team in the opening candlelight ceremony, she is more than likely to have a tear in her eye. Her loyal supporters will be behind her every step of the way.

A But the Championships are different because there's only one chance and you have to be ready to make the most of it.

B In fact, some of them help me with my speed and ball-skills training.

C But once the final whistle blows, you become a different person.

D So I took the decision some time ago that this competition would be the end of it as far as playing is concerned.

E I'm on a strict timetable to gain maximum fitness for them.

F As far as I'm aware, we have always beaten them, but they'll be exciting to play.

G As captain, I think it's important that I have a strong mental attitude and lead by example.

H As a result of playing here, there will be more pressure than we're used to.

Part 3

You are going to read a magazine article about five young designers. For questions **16–30**, choose from the designers (**A–E**). The designers may be chosen more than once. When more than one answer is required, these may be given in any order.

Mark your answers **on the separate answer sheet**.

Which designer(s)

advises against certain styles?

16	

took a business decision based on their own personal taste?

17	

had begun designing before being trained?

18	

have adapted a traditional style?

19		20	

works in a variety of environments?

21	

is working with a material which is new to them?

22	

have used their reputation to develop a new area of business?

23		24	

are completely self-taught?

25		26	

mention how tastes have changed recently?

27		28	

have received professional recognition?

29		30	

Style Merchants

Style informs every part of our lives today from clothes to interior decoration and accessories. Jo Foley provides a taste of the trends for this year's followers of fashion.

A Ned Ingham: Dress Designer

Ned Ingham makes dreamy, romantic wedding dresses. 'People would do well to avoid the traditional, rather stiff dresses and the 'frilly' look in favour of much simpler styles,' he explains. Ingham has been drawing and designing wedding dresses since he was a schoolboy. Then, at the age of 16, he enrolled at fashion school, where he gained the technical skills to cut and construct clothes. But you do not have to be a bride to own an Ingham dress: he also designs long, classic evening dresses, given a fresh touch by up-to-the-minute colours and fabrics. For the less adventurous, Ingham's designs include a classic summer navy-blue suit, the centrepiece of the Englishwoman's wardrobe for most of the 20th century. But in his hands, it looks as new as tomorrow.

B Sally Quail: Jeweller

Although she once worked for an art dealer, Sally Quail has had no formal training in jewellery. It was only when she could not find an engagement ring she liked that she decided to design her own. The resulting enquiries encouraged her to set up as a designer in 1990. Now her pieces are sought out by many stars of stage and screen. Her signature style is large semi-precious stones set in gold to make magnificent necklaces, bracelets and rings fashioned after those worn in the 18th century. However, she has recently begun to use the most precious stone of all – diamonds. 'It must reflect my age,' says 36-year-old Quail. 'I reached that moment in every woman's life when she wants a diamond and that is when I began working with them.'

C Lily Grimson: Handbag Designer

Just four years after setting up in the fiercely competitive fashion business, Lily Grimson, with only an introductory course in art and design behind her, has had two of her creations selected for a major design exhibition. Whatever the shape and form of her designs, they are never ignored. All of Grimson's fashion bags are handmade in the UK. The Grimson handbag is not simply a container – the bags are full of glamour, whether fashioned from the finest calfskin or the heaviest silk. A combination of chic and care makes a Grimson bag something special.

D Peter Little: Hairdresser

For over 20 years, Peter Little has taken his scissors to some of the world's top heads. Everyone who is anyone has had their hair styled by this man. 'Most women want real-looking hair and a style they can manage at home,' he says. So his approach is a novel one – to ensure that his clients never appear as if they have just walked out of a salon. But this carefree attitude and casual look does not come cheap – £250 for the first appointment, and there's a three-month waiting list. Trading on his celebrity, Peter has produced his own range of hairdryers and other styling equipment. Now, those who can't make it to his salon can create their own styles back at home.

E Penny Pratt: Florist

In addition to running her tiny shop, Penny Pratt is a flower consultant for a large chain of supermarkets and provides floral ideas to a number of top restaurants. All of this is good going for someone who has no floristry qualifications and gave up her job as a teacher 10 years ago in order to do 'something different'. And her simple, yet incredibly modern, creations have begun to capture every design prize in the flower business, which has helped her in setting up her own London Flower School. She has recently combined her skills on extremely successful lecture trips to Japan and the USA. She says, 'Flower arrangements are much simpler these days. Keep them simple but strong and don't have too many leaves – they are too large and architectural. For wedding bouquets, whatever your arrangement, the golden rule remains: the flowers must be of the same species.'

PAPER 2 WRITING (1 hour 20 minutes)

Part 1

You **must** answer this question. Write your answer in **120–150** words in an appropriate style.

1   You are helping to organise a visit to a college in an English-speaking country for a group of students. You have received a letter from Michael Slater, the College Director. Read the letter and the notes you have made. Then write a letter to Mr Slater using **all** your notes.

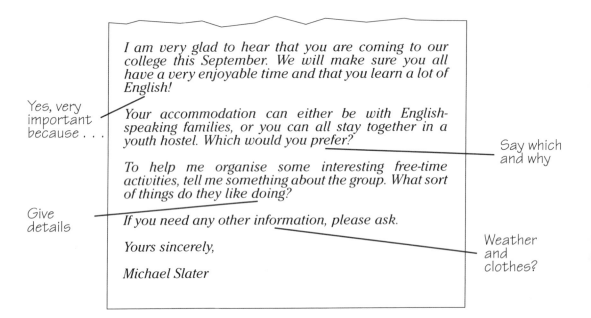

Yes, very important because . . .

I am very glad to hear that you are coming to our college this September. We will make sure you all have a very enjoyable time and that you learn a lot of English!

Your accommodation can either be with English-speaking families, or you can all stay together in a youth hostel. Which would you prefer?

Say which and why

To help me organise some interesting free-time activities, tell me something about the group. What sort of things do they like doing?

Give details

If you need any other information, please ask.

Yours sincerely,

Michael Slater

Weather and clothes?

Write your **letter**. You must use grammatically correct sentences with accurate spelling and punctuation in a style appropriate for the situation.

Do not write any postal addresses.

Part 2

Write an answer to **one** of the questions **2–5** in this part. Write your answer in **120–180** words in an appropriate style.

---

2   Your English class has done a project on transport. Your teacher has now asked you to write an essay giving your opinions on the following statement.

There is no future for public transport because travelling by car is so much more convenient.

Write your **essay**.

3   You see this announcement in your school English-language magazine.

> ### New Clubs after School
>
> Your school wants to start some new after-school clubs. Chess, table tennis, guitar playing and cookery have been suggested as possible ideas for clubs. What do you think? Write us an article for the school magazine.
> - Tell us which one of these four ideas you like best **and** why.
> - Make one other suggestion for a new club **and** explain why it would be a good idea.

Write your **article**.

4   You recently saw this notice in an international travel magazine.

> ## Reviews needed
>
> We would like our readers to send us reviews of good or bad hotels. Write about a hotel anywhere in the world. In your review, describe the hotel and say why you did or did not enjoy staying there.
>
> We will publish the most interesting reviews.

Write your **review**.

5   Answer **one** of the following two questions based on **one** of the titles below.

(a) *Officially Dead* – Richard Prescott

You have had a class discussion on the robbery in *Officially Dead*. Now your teacher has asked you to write an essay answering this question:

*'Why did the police suspect John and Linda Bentley **and** how were they eventually caught?'*

Write your **essay**.

(b) *Pride and Prejudice* – Jane Austen

You have received this letter from your English penfriend, Greg.

> *Pride and Prejudice* has so many different characters! Which person do you feel the most sympathy for and why? Write and tell me.
> Greg

Write your **letter** to Greg.

PAPER 3   USE OF ENGLISH (45 minutes)

Part 1

For questions **1–12**, read the text below and decide which answer (**A, B, C** or **D**) best fits each gap. There is an example at the beginning (**0**).

Mark your answers **on the separate answer sheet**.

Example:

0   A   learn   **B**   capture   **C**   discover   **D**   get

0	A	B	C	D

Learning to make a perfect pizza

According to the European Pizza-Makers' Association, making a good pizza is not a straightforward skill to **(0)** .... The ingredients seem very simple: flour, yeast, water and a bit of salt. **(1)** ...... , water and flour can easily **(2)** ..... a rather unappetizing gluey mix, and anyone who has eaten a **(3)** ..... quality pizza will know how bad it can make your stomach **(4)** ....

'In Italy, 70 per cent of pizza makers could improve on their product, not to **(5)** ..... all the pizza makers around the world who **(6)** ..... uneatable meals,' says Antonio Primiceri, the Association's founder. He has now started a pizza school in an attempt to **(7)** ..... the reputation of this traditional dish. As part of an **(8)** ..... course, the students at Mr Primiceri's school are taught to **(9)** ..... common mistakes, produce a good basic mixture, add a tasty topping and cook the pizza properly. 'Test the finished pizza by breaking the crust,' advises Mr Primiceri. 'If the soft **(10)** ..... inside the pizza is white, clean and dry, it's a good pizza. If it is not like this, the pizza will **(11)** ..... your stomach. You will feel **(12)** ..... full and also thirsty.'

1 **A** However   **B** Despite   **C** Although   **D** Conversely

2 **A** make out   **B** take up   **C** put out   **D** turn into

3 **A** sad   **B** poor   **C** short   **D** weak

4 **A** sense   **B** do   **C** feel   **D** be

5 **A** state   **B** mention   **C** remark   **D** tell

6 **A** submit   **B** give   **C** provide   **D** deal

7 **A** save   **B** hold   **C** deliver   **D** return

8 **A** extensive   **B** extreme   **C** intensive   **D** intentional

9 **A** pass   **B** escape   **C** miss   **D** avoid

10 **A** spot   **B** part   **C** side   **D** slice

11 **A** worry   **B** upset   **C** ache   **D** depress

12 **A** discouragingly **B** tightly   **C** uncomfortably **D** heavily

Part 2

For questions **13–24**, read the text below and think of the word which best fits each gap. Use only **one** word in each gap. There is an example at the beginning (**0**).

Write your answers **IN CAPITAL LETTERS on the separate answer sheet**.

Example:

0	I	T																		

Hollywood

How was (**0**) ......it......that Hollywood came to be the place everyone associates with the American film industry?

In 1887, Harvey Wilcox, a property developer, bought a house and all the surrounding land on a hillside in southern California. His wife overheard a woman talking on a train about her summer house, (**13**) .... she called 'Hollywood'. Mrs Wilcox liked the name (**14**) .... much that she decided to give her new home (**15**) .... same name. Mr Wilcox then built other houses on his land and used the name for the whole community.

In normal circumstances most people (**16**) .... never have heard of Hollywood. But between 1908 and 1913 (**17**) .... else happened. Many small independent film companies began moving to southern California (**18**) .... two main reasons. Firstly, they were having problems (**19**) .... the larger, more powerful studios in New York. Secondly, they were attracted by the sunny climate, which let them film throughout the year (**20**) .... the need for expensive lighting.

Only one studio actually set (**21**) ..r........ in Hollywood itself, because the local people took legal measures (**22**) ..TO.... prevent any more from arriving. The other studios that came to the area were all built outside Hollywood. Nevertheless, by 1915 'Hollywood' (**23**) ....e become familiar as a term for the movie business (**24**) .... a whole.

Part 3

For questions **25–34**, read the text below. Use the word given in capitals at the end of some of the lines to form a word that fits in the gap **in the same line**. There is an example at the beginning **(0)**.

Write your answers **IN CAPITAL LETTERS on the separate answer sheet**.

Example:

0	M	E	E	T	I	N	G									

A new supermarket for the town

At a public **(0)** ...meeting.. held recently, residents of the town of Oxwell **MEET**

met local politicians and shop owners to discuss plans to build a large

supermarket in the town. A wide **(25)** .... of opinions was **VARY**

expressed, some in favour and some against the project. A

(26) .... of the supermarket group, who was present at the meeting, **DIRECT**

stated that the supermarket would benefit the **(27)** .... of **INHABIT**

Oxwell as it would give people more **(28)** .... when shopping. He **CHOOSE**

also pointed out that it would lead to a **(29)** .... in the number of **GROW**

jobs available in the town, which has a high rate of **(30)** .... **EMPLOY**

Although there was general **(31)** .... on the need for new jobs, **AGREE**

some of those present claimed that the presence of the proposed new

supermarket would actually lead to the **(32)** .... of jobs. They **LOSE**

pointed out that small shops would be forced to close as they would

be **(33)** .... to compete with supermarket prices. The final **ABLE**

(34) .... on whether or not to build the supermarket will be made **DECIDE**

next month.

Part 4

For questions **35–42**, complete the second sentence so that it has a similar meaning to the first sentence, using the word given. **Do not change the word given**. You must use between **two** and **five** words, including the word given. Here is an example (**0**).

Example:

0   You must do exactly what the manager tells you.

CARRY

You must .... instructions exactly.

The gap can be filled by the words 'carry out the manager's', so you write:

| **Example:** | **0** | *CARRY OUT THE MANAGER'S* |

Write **only** the missing words **IN CAPITAL LETTERS on the separate answer sheet**.

---

35   We had to finish all the work before we could leave.

UNTIL

We had to stay .... all the work.

36   Tim had not expected the concert to be so good.

BETTER

The concert .... had expected.

37   If Cheryl doesn't train harder, she'll never get into the swimming team.

DOES

Cheryl will never get into the swimming team .... more training.

38   'Do you realise what the time is, Steve?' asked Chris.

WHAT

Chris asked Steve .... it was.

39 The company decided to advertise the job in a national newspaper.

PUT

The company decided to .... the job in a national newspaper.

40 At the end of his speech, the winner thanked his parents.

FINISHED

The winner .... his parents.

41 I applied for the job a month ago.

MONTH

It .... I applied for the job.

42 They received many letters of support after they had appeared on television.

FOLLOWING

They received many letters of support .... on television.

PAPER 4   LISTENING (approximately 40 minutes)

Part 1

You will hear people talking in eight different situations. For questions **1–8**, choose the best answer (**A**, **B** or **C**).

1   You hear part of a radio play.
    Where is the scene taking place?

    A   in the street

    B   in a bank

    C   in a police station

2   You overhear the beginning of a lecture.
    What subject are the students taking?

    A   medicine

    B   sport

    C   music

3   You overhear a conversation in a college.
    Who is the young man?

    A   a new student

    B   a student in the middle of a course

    C   a former student

4   You hear a woman on the radio talking about a cookbook.
    What does she regret?

    A   not looking after it

    B   not having kept it

    C   not using it properly

5 You hear someone talking about the day he met someone famous.
How did he feel after meeting Chris Turner?

    A   unimpressed with the footballer

    B   angry with his friend

    C   disappointed with himself

6 You hear a woman talking on the phone.
Why has she called?

    A   to request a meeting

    B   to offer assistance

    C   to apologise for her absence

7 You overhear an extract from a radio play.
What is the young woman's relationship with the man?

    A   She's a pupil of his.

    B   She's a relative of his.

    C   She's a patient of his.

8 You hear someone telling a story about a strange thing that happened in the mountains.
What point does the story prove?

    A   how strange things can be explained simply

    B   how easy it is to imagine things

    C   how you can be tricked by the silence

Part 2

You will hear part of a talk about dolls. For questions **9–18**, complete the sentences.

Dolls

The first known dolls were found in | 9 | in ancient Egypt.

The earliest dolls in the museum date from the | 10

Early European dolls were dressed like | 11

On the 17th-century dolls, you can see details like the | 12

17th-century dolls may cost as much as | 13 | each.

Collectors look for examples in perfect condition, with their

| 14

19th-century dolls had | 15 | and real hair.

If you can take off the doll's hair, you may see the

| 16 | underneath.

Before the 20th century, all dolls were | 17 |, not babies.

From the 1930s, dolls were made of | 18

Part 3

You will hear five different people talking about why they decided to become nurses. For questions **19–23**, choose which of the reasons (**A–F**) each speaker is giving. Use the letters only once. There is one extra letter which you do not need to use.

A It was a childhood dream.

Speaker 1 | **19**

B Teachers had recommended it.

Speaker 2 | **20**

C A friend had decided to do it.

Speaker 3 | **21**

D It offered a secure income.

Speaker 4 | **22**

E It is a family tradition.

Speaker 5 | **23**

F It is emotionally satisfying.

Part 4

You will hear an interview with someone who works in the film industry. For questions **24–30**, choose the best answer (**A**, **B** or **C**).

24 What does Alan say about his job title?

   A   It confuses a lot of people.

   B   It is just a name for the job.

   C   It encourages him to work hard.

25 Alan considers his job to be

   A   creative.

   B   managerial.

   C   administrative.

26 When he started in films, Alan

   A   immediately learnt new skills.

   B   did the same kind of work as before.

   C   had to change his working methods.

27 When Alan was working on his latest film,

   A   problems were caused by the weather.

   B   there were difficulties moving the equipment.

   C   he wished he was in the studio.

28 For Alan, the disadvantage of the job is

   A   the amount of responsibility.

   B   the criticism he receives.

   C   the effect on family life.

29 For a job like this, Alan recommends

    A   studying to be an electrician.

    B   getting a qualification in maths.

    C   doing a course in film production.

30 In thinking about the future, Alan wants to

    A   face different problems.

    B   work in other areas of production.

    C   continue doing the same job.

PAPER 5   SPEAKING (14 minutes)

You take the Speaking test with another candidate, referred to here as your partner. There are two examiners. One will speak to you and your partner and the other will be listening. Both examiners will award marks.

Part 1 (3 minutes)

The examiner asks you and your partner questions about yourselves. You may be asked about things like 'your home town', 'your interests', 'your career plans', etc.

Part 2 (a one-minute 'long turn' for each candidate, plus 20-second response from the second candidate)

The examiner gives you two photographs and asks you to talk about them for one minute. The examiner then asks your partner a question about your photographs and your partner responds briefly.

Then the examiner gives your partner two different photographs. Your partner talks about these photographs for one minute. This time the examiner asks you a question about your partner's photographs and you respond briefly.

Part 3 (approximately 3 minutes)

The examiner asks you and your partner to talk together. You may be asked to solve a problem or try to come to a decision about something. For example, you might be asked to decide the best way to use some rooms in a language school. The examiner gives you a picture to help you but does not join in the conversation.

Part 4 (approximately 4 minutes)

The interlocutor asks some further questions, which leads to a more general discussion of what you have talked about in Part 3. You may comment on your partner's answers if you wish.

Test 2

PAPER 1   READING (1 hour)

Part 1

You are going to read an extract from a novel. For questions **1–8**, choose the answer (**A**, **B**, **C** or **D**) which you think fits best according to the text.

Mark your answers **on the separate answer sheet**.

O̱n Saturday mornings I worked in the family shop. I started cycling down to the shop with Dad on Saturdays as soon as I was big enough. I thought of it as giving him a hand and so I didn't mind what I did, although it was mostly just fetching and carrying at a run all morning. I managed not to think of it as work and I looked forward to the bar of chocolate my grandmother passed me unsmilingly as I left. I tried not to look at her; I had reason to feel guilty because I'd generally already eaten some dried fruits or a sliver of cheese when no one was looking. As soon as I was fifteen, though, Dad said, 'That's it, our Janet. You're of working age now and you're not coming to work unless your grandmother pays you properly.' He did his best to make his chin look determined. 'I shall speak to her.'

The next Saturday, Gran called me into her little office behind the shop. I always hated going in there. She had an electric heater on full blast, and the windows were always kept tightly closed whatever the weather. There were piles of dusty catalogues and brochures on the floor. 'You're wanting to get paid, I hear,' Gran said. 'Yes, please,' I replied. It was rather like visiting the headmistress at school, so I was very quiet and respectful. Gran searched through the mess of papers on her crowded desk, sighing and clicking her tongue. Eventually she produced an official-looking leaflet and ran her fingers along the columns of figures. 'How old are you?' 'Fifteen ... Gran,' I added for extra politeness, but she looked at me as if I had been cheeky. 'Full-timers at your age get forty pounds for a thirty-five-hour week,' she announced in such a way as to leave no doubt that she
19 wasn't in favour of this. 'No wonder there's no profit in shopkeeping! So, Janet, what's that per
20 hour?' Questions like that always flustered me. Instead of trying to work them out in my head, I would just stand there, unable to think straight. 'I'll get a pencil and paper,' I offered. 'Don't bother,' snapped Gran angrily, 'I'll do it myself. I'll give you a pound an hour; take it or leave it.' 'I'll take it, please.' 'And I expect real work for it, mind. No standing about, and if I catch you eating any of the stock, there'll be trouble. That's theft, and it's a crime.'

From then on, my main job at the shop was filling the shelves. This was dull, but I hardly expected to be trusted with handling the money. Once or twice, however, when Dad was extra busy, I'd tried to help him by serving behind the counter. I hated it. It was very difficult to remember the prices of everything and I was particularly hopeless at using the till. Certain customers made unkind remarks about this, increasing my confusion and the chances of my making a fool of myself.

It was an old-established village shop, going back 150 years at least and it was really behind the times even then. Dad longed to be able to make the shop more attractive to customers, but Gran wouldn't hear of it. I overheard them once arguing about whether to buy a freezer cabinet. 'Our customers want frozen food,' Dad said. 'They see things advertised and if they can't get them from us, they'll go elsewhere.' 'Your father always sold fresh food,' Gran replied. 'People come here for quality, they don't want all that frozen stuff.'

Actually, she gave way in the end over the freezer. Mr Timson, her great rival, installed one in his shop at the other end of the village and customers started making loud comments about how handy it was, being able to get frozen food in the village, and how good Mr Timson's sausages were. That really upset her because she was proud of her sausages and she ungraciously gave Dad the money to buy the freezer. Within a couple of weeks, she was eating frozen food like the rest of us.

1   How did Janet feel when she first started her Saturday morning job?

    A   She enjoyed the work that she was given.
    B   She was pleased to be helping her father.
    C   She worried that she was not doing it well.
    D   She was only really interested in the reward.

2   What do we learn about her grandmother's office in the second paragraph?

    A   It needed decorating.
    B   It was untidy.
    C   It had too much furniture in it.
    D   It was dark.

3   'This' (line 19) refers to

    A   shopkeepers' profits.
    B   a thirty-five-hour week.
    C   Janet's request.
    D   the recommended wage.

4   'Flustered' (line 20) means

    A   bored.
    B   angered.
    C   confused.
    D   depressed.

5   Why did Janet's grandmother react angrily to her offer to fetch a pencil and paper?

    A   Janet was unable to answer her question.
    B   Janet had been unwilling to help her.
    C   Janet had made an unhelpful suggestion.
    D   Janet had answered her rudely.

6   What did Janet's father and grandmother disagree about?

    A   how to keep their customers loyal to the shop
    B   the type of advertising needed to attract customers
    C   the type of customers they needed to attract
    D   how to get new customers to come to the shop

7   What eventually persuaded Janet's grandmother to buy a freezer?

    A   She found that she liked frozen food after all.
    B   A new shop opening in the village had one.
    C   It was suggested that her products weren't fresh.
    D   She responded to pressure from her customers.

8   What impression do we get of Janet's feelings towards her grandmother?

    A   She respected her fairness.
    B   She doubted her judgement.
    C   She disliked her manner.
    D   She admired her determination.

Part 2

You are going to read an article written by someone who lives in a house in a valley. Seven sentences have been removed from the article. Choose from the sentences **A–H** the one which fits each gap (**9–15**). There is one extra sentence which you do not need to use.

Mark your answers **on the separate answer sheet**.

LIVING IN THE VALLEY

We had been living in our valley for sixteen months when we first realised the dangers that could exist in the surrounding hills and threaten our very survival.

9   Until that time, we had felt safe and sheltered in our valley below the protecting hills.

Soon snow began to fall. Within a day it lay some 15 centimetres deep. **10**   But on the neighbouring heights the snow was much deeper and stayed for longer. Up there the wind blasted fiercely. Deep in our valley we felt only sudden gusts of wind; trees swayed but the branches held firm.

And yet we knew that there was reason for us to worry. The snow and wind were certainly inconvenient but they did not really trouble us greatly. **11**   It reminded us of what could have occurred if circumstances had been different, if the flow of water from the hills had not, many years before, been controlled, held back by a series of dams.

In a short time the snow started to melt. Day after day, we watched furious clouds pile up high over the hills to the west. Sinister grey clouds extended over the valleys. **12**   We had seen enough of the sky; now we began to watch the river, which every day was becoming fuller and wilder.

The snow was gradually washed away as more and more rain streamed from the clouds, but high up in the hills the reservoir was filling and was fast approaching danger level. And then it happened – for the first time in years the reservoir overflowed. **13**

The river seemed maddened as the waters poured almost horizontally down to its lower stretches. Just a couple of metres from our cottage, the stream seemed wild beneath the bridge. **14**   For three days we prayed that it would stay below its wall. Fortunately, our prayers were answered as the dam held and the waters began to subside.

On many occasions through the centuries before the dam was built, the river had flooded the nearby villages in just such a rage. Now, though, the dam restricts the flow of the river and usually all is well; the great mass of water from the hills, the product of snow and torrential rain, remains behind its barrier with just the occasional overflow. **15**   Thanks to this protection we can feel our home in the valley is still secure and safe.

A   It was the river, the Ryburn, which normally flowed so gently, that threatened us most. *Rive*

B   And yet the immense power of all this water above us prevents us from ever believing ourselves to be completely safe in our home.

C   They twisted and turned, rising eastwards and upwards, warning of what was to come. *Co*

D   It was far deeper than we'd ever seen it so near our home, lunging furiously at its banks.

E   We can thus enjoy, rather than fear, the huge clouds that hang over the valley, and can be thrilled by the tremendous power which we know the river possesses.

F   It almost completely blocked our lane and made the streamside path slippery and dangerous.

G   There in the heights it was like the Niagara Falls, as the water surged over the edge of the dam and poured into the stream below.

H   It was the year when the storms came early, before the calendar even hinted at winter, even before November was out.

Part 3

You are going to read a magazine article in which five people talk about their characters. For questions **16–30**, choose from the people (**A–E**). The people may be chosen more than once. When more than one answer is required, these may be given in any order.

Mark your answers **on the separate answer sheet**.

Which person or people state(s) the following?

I used to avoid giving my opinions at work.	**16**
Taking time off for your professional development can make you feel more self-assured.	**17**
I never thought I'd be a confident person.	**18**
I'm not influenced by people's opinions of me.	**19**
Everyone gets nervous at times.	**20** · **21**
Initially, I misunderstood what confidence was.	**22**
I find making notes very supportive in my work.	**23**
A certain event changed the course of my life.	**24** · **25**
I've worked on having a confident appearance.	**26**
I am realistic about my abilities.	**27** · **28**
My behaviour helps others relax too.	**29**
Getting things wrong can have a positive result.	**30**

Confident people
What's their secret?

Confident people may look as though they were born that way, but most will tell you that it's a skill they've learned because they had to. Nina Hathway asks five people how they did it.

A Jenny

When I left school I was very shy and I always thought I'd stay that way. I was about twenty-five when I was asked to help out at my daughter's school. I was sure I wouldn't cope, but I surprised myself by doing well and someone there suggested that I should do a university course.

There was a huge knot in my stomach the day I turned up for my first lecture. But my confidence gradually grew – I became more outgoing. Looking back, working at the school was the turning point in my life that has helped everything else fall into place.

B Michaela

It all started four years ago when my father became ill and I had to take over the family business. I was so scared, I went over the top and became a bit too aggressive and impatient. I thought that was what confident people were like, but gradually I learned otherwise. To be confident you've got to believe in yourself.

If things get too demanding for me at work, I don't let myself feel guilty if I save a number of tasks until the next day. When I'm confronted with something difficult, I tell myself that I've got nothing to lose. It's fear that makes you lack confidence, so I'm always having quiet chats with myself to put aside those fears!

C Lisa

People think I'm very confident but, in fact, the calmer I look, the more terrified I really am. I've had to develop the ability to look confident because it's the most vital thing in TV. Interviewing people has helped me realise that most – if not all – of us get tense in important situations, and we feel calmer when we speak to someone who's genuinely friendly. The best ever piece of advice came from my mother when I was agonising as a teenager about wearing the right clothes. She simply cried, 'Who's looking at you? Everybody's too busy worrying about how they look.' I've found that's well worth remembering.

I also think you gain confidence by tackling things that scare you. When I took my driving test I was so nervous, but I passed. After that I felt sure that I'd never feel so frightened again, and I never have.

D Barbara

My confidence comes naturally from really enjoying the work I do, but it's something that I've built up over the years. If you just get on with it and learn from any mistakes you make, you're more confident the next time round. I work hard and I'm popular in the restaurant, but it's probable that one out of ten people doesn't like me. I don't let that affect me. You've got to like yourself for what you are, not try to be what others expect.

My company runs a lot of training courses, and going on those has built up my self-esteem. The company also encourages employees to set manageable targets. It helps no end if you can see you're achieving something tangible, rather than reaching for the stars all at once, and ending up with nothing but air!

E Kim

After I left college I worked for years as a secretary and would sit in meetings, not always agreeing with what was being said, but too scared to speak up. Eventually, I summoned up the confidence to start making my point. Even so, when I first worked in politics, I'd never spoken in public before and always used to shake like a leaf. I would say to myself, 'Don't be so silly. People do this every day of their lives, so there's no reason why you can't.' I also found it helpful to jot a few things down to refer to – rather like having a comfort blanket!

I don't think there is anyone who isn't a little shaky when it comes to talking publicly. The real secret of confidence lies in telling yourself over and over again, 'Nothing is impossible.'

PAPER 2   WRITING (1 hour 20 minutes)

Part 1

You **must** answer this question. Write your answer in **120–150** words in an appropriate style.

---

1   Your English friend, Peter, has sent you an email asking you to help him organise a special
surprise birthday party for his sister, Anna. Read Peter's email and the notes you have made.
Then write an email to Peter using **all** your notes.

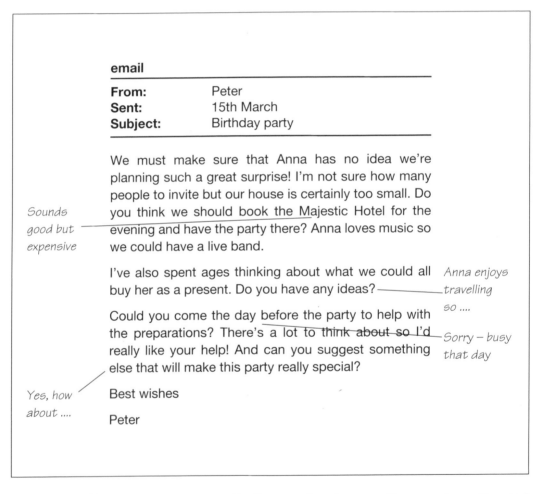

email

From:	Peter
Sent:	15th March
Subject:	Birthday party

We must make sure that Anna has no idea we're planning such a great surprise! I'm not sure how many people to invite but our house is certainly too small. Do you think we should book the Majestic Hotel for the evening and have the party there? Anna loves music so we could have a live band.

Sounds good but expensive

I've also spent ages thinking about what we could all buy her as a present. Do you have any ideas?

Anna enjoys travelling so ....

Could you come the day before the party to help with the preparations? There's a lot to think about so I'd really like your help! And can you suggest something else that will make this party really special?

Sorry – busy that day

Best wishes

Peter

Yes, how about ....

Write your **email**. You must use grammatically correct sentences with accurate spelling and punctuation in a style appropriate for the situation.

Part 2

Write an answer to **one** of the questions **2–5** in this part. Write your answer in **120–180** words in an appropriate style.

---

2   You have had a discussion on fashion in your English class. Your teacher has now asked you to write an essay, giving your opinions on the following statement:

Young people always want to dress differently from their parents.

Write your **essay**.

3   You have seen this advertisement for a job in the USA in an international magazine.

> **USA SUMMER CAMPS**
>
> If you can speak English and you are cheerful, energetic and hardworking, you are the right person for us. Food and accommodation are provided. You just pay the air fare.
>
> You will   – look after children aged 8 –12
>   – help organise sports and evening activities
>   – work in the kitchens
>
> Write to the director, Mrs Connor, and explain why you would be a suitable person for the job.

Write your **application**.

4   Your teacher has asked you to write a story for an international student magazine. The story must **begin** with the following words:

Michael closed the door and knew at that moment he had made a mistake.

Write your **story**.

5   Answer **one** of the following two questions based on **one** of the titles below.

(a) *Officially Dead* – Richard Prescott

You have seen this announcement in an English magazine.

> **TRUTH and LIES**
>
> We are looking for articles about books where telling the truth or lies is important to the story. The best articles will be published next month.

Write an **article** about the importance of truth and lies in *Officially Dead*.

(b) *Pride and Prejudice* – Jane Austen

Your English class has discussed the characters of Lizzy and Mr Darcy in *Pride and Prejudice*. Your teacher has now given you this essay for homework:

Explain how and why Lizzy's feelings for Mr Darcy change.

Write your **essay**.

PAPER 3   USE OF ENGLISH (45 minutes)

Part 1

For questions **1–12**, read the text below and decide which answer (**A, B, C** or **D**) best fits each gap. There is an example at the beginning (**0**).

Mark your answers **on the separate answer sheet**.

Example:

0   A   celebrates   **B**   shows   **C**   honours   **D**   demonstrates

0	A	B	C	D
	▬	—	—	—

Everyone's an artist

Every year, the village of Pettineo **(0)** ..... its unique arts festival. For a few days each summer, artists from all over Europe **(1)** ..... at this village near the north coast of Sicily to **(2)** ..... the creative atmosphere. During their stay, the artists get together with the local people to paint a one-kilometre long picture that runs the **(3)** ..... of the high street. **(4)** ..... the painting is done, each visiting artist joins a local family for a big lunch and, **(5)** ..... the meal, the family receives the **(6)** ..... of the painting that the artist has painted. As a result, **(7)** ..... few villagers are rich, almost every home has at least one painting by a well-known European artist. Visitors to the village are eagerly **(8)** ..... into homes to see these paintings.

The festival was the idea of Antonio Presti, a local businessman who **(9)** ..... it up several years ago. Since then, Pettineo has **(10)** ..... a sort of domestic art museum in **(11)** ..... any visitor can ring a doorbell, go into a house and **(12)** ..... a painting. In addition to this exhibition of paintings in people's homes, for those who have time to spare, there is an opportunity to wander through the display of huge sculptures in the village square.

1 **A** group   **B** crowd   **C** gather   **D** combine

2 **A** amuse   **B** enjoy   **C** entertain   **D** delight ?

3 **A** size   **B** measure   **C** length   **D** area

4 **A** Just   **B** Once   **C** Soon   **D** Only

5 **A** in addition to   **B** in place of   **C** in common with   **D** in exchange for

6 **A** partition   **B** section   **C** division   **D** region

7 **A** though   **B** despite   **C** since   **D** even

8 **A** persuaded   **B** invited   **C** requested   **D** attracted ?

9 **A** set   **B** put   **C** got   **D** had

10 **A** become   **B** advanced   **C** grown   **D** increased

11 **A** what   **B** where   **C** whom   **D** which

12 **A** wonder   **B** stare   **C** admire   **D** respect

Part 2

For questions **13–24**, read the text below and think of the word which best fits each gap. Use only **one** word in each gap. There is an example at the beginning (**0**).

Write your answers **IN CAPITAL LETTERS on the separate answer sheet.**

Example: | 0 | W | I | T | H | | | | | | | | | | | | | |

Problems for actors

Many actors do not like working **(0)** ...with... children or animals. This is probably **(13)** .... they are afraid that the audience may become **(14)** .... interested in the children and animals than in them.

Actors can have problems **(15)** .... a different kind when they are required to eat or drink on stage. If they have **(16)** .... much food in their mouths, the words they say may not **(17)** .... clear, and they may even end up coughing or choking.

Other problems can occur with food **(18)** .... films are being made. In a recent film, during **(19)** .... a family was waiting to have a meal, one of the actors entered with a large roast chicken on a tray and started cutting some meat from it while he was speaking. Having cut off a whole chicken leg he completely forgot **(20)** .... his next words were. The scene had to be filmed **(21)** .... This would not really have mattered **(22)** .... there had been another roast chicken in the studio, but there was not. At **(23)** ...., nobody knew what to do, but eventually the problem was solved **(24)** .... putting a nail in the leg and attaching it back onto the chicken.

Part 3

For questions **25–34**, read the text below. Use the word given in capitals at the end of some of the lines to form a word that fits in the gap **in the same line**. There is an example at the beginning (**0**).

Write your answers **IN CAPITAL LETTERS on the separate answer sheet**.

Example: | **0** | G | R | O | W | T | H | | | | | | | | | | |

Airports

Because of the recent (**0**) ..*growth*.. in air travel, airports have become more   **GROW**

than ever before symbols of international importance. They therefore have

to look good and are (**25**) ………. designed by well-known architects. In   **FREQUENT**

addition to this, competition and customer demand mean that airports

generally have to have (**26**) ………. facilities nowadays. For instance,   **IMPRESS**

there are (**27**) ………. departure lounges, where passengers can wait   **COMFORT**

before their (**28**) ………. takes off, luxurious restaurants, shopping areas   **FLY**

and banks. Good road and rail (**29**) ………. with nearby towns and cities   **CONNECT**

are also essential, with large numbers of people needing to get to and from

the airport quickly and efficiently.

However, it is becoming (**30**) ………. difficult to find land on which to   **INCREASE**

build airports. One reason for this is that aircraft, despite (**31**) ……….   **IMPROVE**

in engine design, are still very (**32**) ………. , and need a considerable   **NOISE**

amount of space in which to land and take off. This of course means

that (**33**) ………. residential areas need to be avoided, so,   **CROWD**

(**34**) ………. , travellers often find that the airport they need to use might   **FORTUNATE**

be situated at an inconvenient distance from the city.

Part 4

For questions **35–42**, complete the second sentence so that it has a similar meaning to the first sentence, using the word given. **Do not change the word given**. You must use between **two** and **five** words, including the word given. Here is an example (**0**).

Example:

0 You must do exactly what the manager tells you.

CARRY

You must .... instructions exactly.

The gap can be filled by the words 'carry out the manager's', so you write:

Example: | **0** | *CARRY OUT THE MANAGER'S* |

Write **only** the missing words **IN CAPITAL LETTERS on the separate answer sheet**.

---

35 John is interested in knowing more about astronomy.

LIKE

John .... more about astronomy.

36 Because of the parade, we weren't allowed to park in the High Street.

LET

Because of the parade, the police wouldn't .... in the High Street.

37 'Did you see that film on television on Saturday?' Susan asked me.

SEEN

Susan wanted to know .... that film on television on Saturday.

38 'I'm afraid these jeans have a hole in them,' Tania told the shop assistant.

THERE

'I'm afraid that .... these jeans,' Tania told the shop assistant.

39 Dan never takes any notice of my advice.

ATTENTION

Dan never .... my advice.

40 'Can I borrow your bicycle, Sarah?' asked Frank.

LEND

Frank asked Sarah .... her bicycle.

41 Maybe Peter forgot that we changed the time of the meeting.

MIGHT

Peter .... that we changed the time of the meeting.

42 All the children enjoy themselves at this summer camp.

FUN

Every .... at this summer camp.

PAPER 4   LISTENING (approximately 40 minutes)

Part 1

You will hear people talking in eight different situations. For questions **1–8**, choose the best answer (**A**, **B** or **C**).

1   You overhear two people talking in a restaurant.
    Where has the woman just come from?

    A   a supermarket

    B   a hospital

    C   a football match

2   You hear a man talking about a mobile phone he has bought.
    What most attracted him to this phone?

    A   its size

    B   its reliability

    C   its price

3   You hear a man talking on the phone about buying a house.
    What is the purpose of his call?

    A   to apologise

    B   to complain

    C   to obtain information

4   You hear a teenage girl talking about her hobby.
    What is she talking about?

    A   a computer game

    B   a musical instrument

    C   a piece of sports equipment

5 On the news, you hear a story about a cat.
Where was the cat found?

  A in a train carriage

  B on the railway lines

  C on a station platform

6 You hear a woman talking about how she gets ideas for her work.
Who is the woman?

  A a novelist

  B an artist

  C a film-maker

7 You hear two people talking.
How does the woman feel?

  A surprised

  B satisfied

  C relieved

8 You turn on the radio and hear a man speaking.
What are you listening to?

  A a history programme

  B a science-fiction story

  C an advertisement

Part 2

You will hear part of a radio programme about bags for walkers. For questions **9–18**, complete the sentences.

Bags for walkers

Rod's shop sells bags and other [**9**] equipment.

A backpack could spoil your holiday if it doesn't [**10**]

A 35-litre bag is good for [**11**]

An upright bag is recommended for people who are going to [**12**]

To protect breakable items choose a bag with a [**13**]

A bag with [**14**] inside will allow you to separate your belongings.

External pockets can be used to carry tools that are [**15**] or dirty.

It is important that shoulder straps are [**16**]

A horizontal bar will prevent shoulder straps from [**17**]

Padded parts of the bag should have plenty of [**18**] so that sweat can escape.

Part 3

You will hear five different students who are studying away from home. They are talking about their accommodation. For questions **19–23**, choose from the list (**A–F**) what each speaker says about their accommodation. Use the letters only once. There is one extra letter which you do not need to use.

A I made a mistake there at first.

Speaker 1 [   ] **19**

B I was able to settle into a new area.

Speaker 2 [   ] **20**

C I had no choice in the matter.

Speaker 3 [   ] **21**

D I have recommended it to others.

Speaker 4 [   ] **22**

E There are more benefits than disadvantages.

Speaker 5 [   ] **23**

F I would prefer to have more freedom.

Part 4

You will hear part of a radio interview in which Tina White, a magazine editor, talks about her life and work. For questions **24–30**, choose the best answer (**A**, **B** or **C**).

24 In her first column, Tina chose to write about people who

    A   were very well known.

    B   had interesting ideas.

    C   lived in luxury.

25 She took up journalism because of

    A   her family connections.

    B   her father's support.

    C   her love for books.

26 Under her management, the magazine *Female Focus*

    A   reduced its losses.

    B   changed its image.

    C   made a profit.

27 She believes people are more likely to read an article if

    A   it has a good beginning.

    B   its content is challenging.

    C   it is mentioned on the cover.

28 When she started her present job five years ago, she

    A   organised her ideal team.

    B   had more time to read everything.

    C   lacked confidence in her staff.

29 Tina says that she would be worried if she

    A   was criticised by the public.

    B   lost the respect of colleagues.

    C   lost her job.

30 In the future, she would like to

    A   be a book editor.

    B   produce a film.

    C   write fiction.

PAPER 5   SPEAKING (14 minutes)

You take the Speaking test with another candidate, referred to here as your partner. There are two examiners. One will speak to you and your partner and the other will be listening. Both examiners will award marks.

Part 1 (3 minutes)

The examiner asks you and your partner questions about yourselves. You may be asked about things like 'your home town', 'your interests', 'your career plans', etc.

Part 2 (a one-minute 'long turn' for each candidate, plus 20-second response from the second candidate)

The examiner gives you two photographs and asks you to talk about them for one minute. The examiner then asks your partner a question about your photographs and your partner responds briefly.

Then the examiner gives your partner two different photographs. Your partner talks about these photographs for one minute. This time the examiner asks you a question about your partner's photographs and you respond briefly.

Part 3 (approximately 3 minutes)

The examiner asks you and your partner to talk together. You may be asked to solve a problem or try to come to a decision about something. For example, you might be asked to decide the best way to use some rooms in a language school. The examiner gives you a picture to help you but does not join in the conversation.

Part 4 (approximately 4 minutes)

The interlocutor asks some further questions, which leads to a more general discussion of what you have talked about in Part 3. You may comment on your partner's answers if you wish.

Test 3

PAPER 1   READING (1 hour)

Part 1

You are going to read an article about a man who makes works of art out of seashells. For questions **1–8**, choose the answer (**A**, **B**, **C** or **D**) which you think fits best according to the text.

Mark your answers **on the separate answer sheet**.

THE SHELL ARTIST

At the age of 83 Peter Cooke has become a master of his art.

There are still many things that Peter Cooke would like to try his hand at – paper-making and feather-work are on his list. For the moment though, he will stick to the skill that he has been delighted to perfect over the past ten years: making delicate and unusual objects out of shells.

'Tell me if I am boring you,' he says, as he leads me round his apartment showing me his work. There is a fine line between being a bore and being an enthusiast, but Cooke need not worry: he fits into the latter category, helped both by his charm and by the beauty of the things he makes.

He points to a pair of shell-covered ornaments above a fireplace. 'I shan't be at all bothered if people don't buy them because I have got so used to them, and to me they're adorable. I never meant to sell my work commercially. Some friends came to see me about five years ago and said, "You must have an exhibition – people ought to see these. We'll talk to a man who owns an art gallery".' The result was an exhibition in London, at which 70 per cent of the objects were sold. His second exhibition opened at the gallery yesterday. Considering the enormous prices the pieces command – around £2,000 for the ornaments – an empty space above the fireplace would seem a small sacrifice for Cooke to make.

There are 86 pieces in the exhibition, with prices starting at £225 for a shell-flower in a crystal vase. Cooke insists that he has nothing to do with the prices and is cheerily open about their level: he claims there is nobody else in the world who produces work like his, and, as the gallery-owner told him, 'Well, you're going to stop one day and everybody will want your pieces because there won't be any more.'

'I do wish, though,' says Cooke, 'that I'd taken this up a lot earlier, because then I would have been able to produce really wonderful things – at least the potential would have been there. Although the ideas are still there and I'm doing the best I can now, I'm more limited physically than I was when I started.' Still, the work that he has managed to produce is a long way from the common shell constructions that can be found in seaside shops. 'I have a miniature mind,' he says, and this has resulted in boxes covered in thousands of tiny shells, little shaded pictures made from shells and baskets of astonishingly realistic flowers.

Cooke has created his own method and uses materials as and when he finds them. He uses the cardboard sent back with laundered shirts for his flower bases, a nameless glue bought in bulk from a sail-maker ('If it runs out, I don't know what I will do!') and washing-up liquid to wash the shells. 'I have an idea of what I want to do, and it just does itself,' he says of his working method, yet the attention to detail, colour gradations and symmetry he achieves look far from accidental.

Cooke's quest for beautiful, and especially tiny, shells has taken him further than his Norfolk shore: to France, Thailand, Mexico, South Africa and the Philippines, to name but a few of the beaches where he has lain on his stomach and looked for beauties to bring home. He is insistent that he only collects dead shells and defends himself against people who write him letters accusing him of stripping the world's beaches. 'When I am collecting shells, I hear people's great fat feet crunching them up far faster than I can collect them; and the ones that are left, the sea breaks up. I would not dream of collecting shells with living creatures in them or diving for them, but once their occupants have left, why should I not collect them?' If one bases this argument on the amount of luggage that can be carried home by one man, the sum beauty of whose work is often greater than its natural parts, it becomes very convincing indeed.

line 25

line 7

1   What does the reader learn about Peter Cooke in the first paragraph?

    A   He has produced hand-made objects in different materials.
    B   He was praised for his shell objects many years ago.
    C   He hopes to work with other materials in the future.
    D   He has written about his love of making shell objects.

2   When looking round his apartment, the writer

    A   is attracted by Cooke's personality.
    B   senses that Cooke wants his products to be admired.
    C   realises he finds Cooke's work boring.
    D   feels uncertain about giving Cooke his opinion.

3   The 'small sacrifice' in line 25 refers to

    A   the loss of Cooke's ornaments.
    B   the display of Cooke's ornaments.
    C   the cost of keeping Cooke's ornaments.
    D   the space required to store Cooke's ornaments.

4   When the writer enquires about the cost of his shell objects, Cooke

    A   cleverly changes the subject.
    B   defends the prices charged for his work.
    C   says he has no idea why the level is so high.
    D   notes that his work will not always be so popular.

5   What does Cooke regret about his work?

    A   He is not as famous as he should have been.
    B   He makes less money than he should make.
    C   He is less imaginative than he used to be.
    D   He is not as skilful as he used to be.

6   When talking about the artist's working method, the writer suspects that Cooke

    A   accepts that he sometimes makes mistakes.
    B   is unaware of the unique quality his work has.
    C   underrates his creative contribution.
    D   undervalues the materials that he uses.

7   What does the reader learn about Cooke's shell-collecting activities?

    A   Not everyone approves of what he does.
    B   Other methods might make his work easier.
    C   Other tourists get in the way of his collecting.
    D   Not all shells are the right size and shape for his work.

8   What does 'it' in line 71 refer to?

    A   Cooke's luggage
    B   Cooke's argument
    C   the beauty of Cooke's work
    D   the reason for Cooke's trips

Part 2

You are going to read a magazine article about a new hotel. Seven sentences have been removed from the article. Choose from the sentences **A–H** the one which fits each gap (**9–15**). There is one extra sentence which you do not need to use.

Mark your answers **on the separate answer sheet**.

Five-star luxury meets up-to-date technology

The five-star Merrion Hotel, which has just opened, is the result of considerable research into customer requirements and nearly two years' work converting four large eighteenth-century houses in Dublin. Creating a new hotel in this way has allowed the latest technology to be installed. This has been done for the benefit of staff and guests alike.

At the Merrion, General Manager Peter MacCann expects his staff to know the guests by name. **9** It can deal with return clients in the extra-special way that is appropriate to a five-star hotel.

Though the system cost £250,000 to install, it will pay for itself over time, according to MacCann. **10** For example, a guest who requests certain music CDs during a first stay will find those same CDs ready for him on a return visit. This is thanks to the guest-history facility which allows staff to key in any number of preferences.

Hotel guests the world over frequently complain about room temperature. **11** Guests have the opportunity to change the temperature themselves within three degrees either side of the normal 18°C but, in addition, each individual room can be adjusted by any amount between 14°C and 25°C at the front desk.

12 This is particularly true for the business user, and MacCann estimates that up to sixty-five per cent of his business will come from this part of the market. To provide the best service for such needs, the hotel has taken the traditional business centre and put it into individual bedrooms. Each one has three phones, two phone lines, a fax machine that doubles as a photocopier and printer, and a video-conferencing facility.

Technology changes so quickly these days that the hotel has had to try to forecast possible improvements. **13** The televisions are rented rather than bought, so that they can be replaced with more up-to-date models at any time. DVD recorders can also be upgraded when necessary.

Despite the presence of all this very up-to-the-minute equipment in the rooms, MacCann says they have tried hard not to make guests feel threatened by the technology. **14** There are, of course, a swimming pool and gym, six conference rooms, two bars and two restaurants, and a beautiful garden at the heart of it all.

As at all luxury hotels, the food that is offered to guests must be excellent. Chef Patrick Guilbaud's Dublin restaurant already had two Michelin stars when he agreed to move his restaurant business to the Merrion. **15** He has been able to design a new kitchen and take it into the modern age. There are better parking facilities than at the previous address, too. From the hotel's side, they are able to offer a popular and successful place to eat, with no financial risks attached.

Aided by technology and a highly capable staff, the Merrion looks likely to succeed.

A For guests, though, it is the other technology offered in their rooms which is most likely to find favour.

B Being part of the hotel site has huge benefits, both for him and the hotel itself.

C Extra cables have been laid to handle whatever scientific advances may occur.

D He expects fifty per cent of the rooms to be occupied in the hotel's first year.

E Another hi-tech system controls this essential area of comfort.

F However, for details of his guests' preferences, he relies on the hotel's computer system.

G The one hundred and forty-five bedrooms, large and well-furnished, are both comfortable and welcoming.

H He praises its efficiency and talks enthusiastically of the facilities it offers.

Part 3

You are going to read a magazine article about members of a part-time drama club called The Globe Players. For questions **16–30**, choose from the people (**A–F**). The people may be chosen more than once. When more than one answer is required, these may be given in any order.

Mark your answers **on the separate answer sheet**.

Which person or people

mentions joining because of loneliness?		**16**
had some theatre experience before joining The Globe Players?		**17**
has a high opinion of The Globe Players?		**18**
joined to keep busy?		**19**
has mixed feelings about finishing a show?		**20**
have difficulty finding suitable roles?	**21**	**22**
enjoys being with people who have different ideas?		**23**
thinks that acting is out of character for them?		**24**
mentions the publicity they sometimes receive?		**25**
believes the other members are like them in character?		**26**
talks about the complications of putting on a play?		**27**
feel that not everyone approves of them acting?	**28**	**29**
doubts their ability to perform?		**30**

The Globe Players

A Christina Howard

When I moved to this area the children were quite little, and I wondered how I was ever going to meet people. Then I met Susanna Dickster, who was the organiser of The Globe Players, and she said, 'Do you want to join?' And I said, 'Well, yes, all right.' They appeared to be incredibly extrovert people, which I suppose I am by nature too. For three years I was the theatre manager. I think I make a better manager than an actress, but I did have a dream role in a play the year before last.

B Eric Plumber

I do about one play a year, just out of interest. But I'm a quiet sort of chap, not one of the world's extroverts, and yet here I am in an extrovert field, doing theatrical activities. There is a sort of magic to the theatre. There's a sense of togetherness with the rest of the actors in the cast. When a play is over, on the last night, there's a combination of anticlimax and relief. It's rather nice to think you will be able to do all the things that you weren't able to do when the play was on. But there's also a sense of loss, so you look forward to the next play.

C Laura Goldcrest

I have done some stage management for productions at my school and when I saw the play The Globe Players were going to do next, I thought I'd try for it. Usually there are not a lot of parts for people my age, so when there was this opportunity, I went along and auditioned. It went all right, and I got the part. Lots of my friends just hang around with people of their own age, but there are people at The Globe Players who are quite old, and I get talking to them about all sorts of things. It's amazing how our views differ, but we have lovely conversations.

D Clare MacDonald

When I was at school, I used to think I'd rather like to go on stage. But then other things came along. One job I did was as a stewardess for an airline. That's like giving a performance. I left the airline and joined The Globe Players. My husband will always come to performances, but he does tend to moan a bit because he feels it takes up too much time. As a club I feel we are very professional. I do about one play a year, which is quite enough for me. Obviously, there are fewer parts as you get older, particularly for women: one can no longer play Juliet or other young parts, which I feel sad about.

E Robin Wilson

I work behind the scenes with The Globe Players because it's always a challenge. For instance, the last play I did needed a full-sized, working swimming pool. Well, most amateur theatres have a bucket of water in the wings. But our director said, 'I want a real swimming pool on that set. Go away and do it.' It was a real challenge for me. However, we did it. We got more reviews than we usually do because, of course, it was something different. And quite a lot of amateur societies came to see if they could do it – and a lot of them decided they couldn't.

F Mike James

I was a science teacher and took early retirement from my college. After twenty-four years it was a bit hard and I got rather bored. During that time it was good to have the drama group. It takes your mind off things; you can't act and worry about something else. But it's very disruptive to a family – my wife will tell you that. Teaching in a way is like being on stage. When you go into a class you may not be feeling very well, you are not necessarily very keen on the subject you are teaching – the whole thing adds up to a no-no. But you go in, you are enthusiastic and you try to generate interest, and it's an act.

PAPER 2   WRITING (1 hour 20 minutes)

Part 1

You **must** answer this question. Write your answer in **120–150** words in an appropriate style.

1   You are studying in Britain and you have recently received a letter from an English friend, Kate, who is interested in arranging a day trip for a group of students. Read Kate's letter, the advertisement and the notes you have made. Then write a letter to Kate, using **all** your notes.

> . . . and the students in my class are really interested in going on a day trip. I know you went on a boat trip with your English class recently. Could you tell me what it was like and whether you'd recommend it?
>
> *Kate*

Castle and Lake Boat Trips

- *Departures 8 a.m. or 10 a.m. daily*

  Less crowded —
- *Stop at Bourne Castle – guided tour*

- *Lunch at restaurant*

  Take a picnic because —
- *Afternoon at lake with choice of water sports* ———— *Try...*

- *Reasonable prices with reductions for groups*

  ———— *Minimum 15 people*

Write your **letter.** You must use grammatically correct sentences with accurate spelling and punctuation in a style appropriate for the situation.

Do not write any postal addresses.

Part 2

Write an answer to **one** of the questions **2–5** in this part. Write your answer in **120–180** words in an appropriate style.

---

2   An English language club is starting in your area. The organisers of the club have asked you to write a report giving your suggestions about:

- how often the club should meet
- what type of activities it should organise
- how the club could be advertised.

Write your **report**.

3   You have decided to enter a short story competition in an international magazine. The competition rules say that the story must **begin** with the following words.

It was three o'clock in the morning when the phone rang.

Write your **story**.

4   You have seen this announcement in *Leisure and Entertainment* magazine.

> ### *Could you live without television for a week?*
>
> Write and tell us what difference this would make to your life.
> We will publish the best article.

Write your **article**.

5   Answer **one** of the following two questions based on **one** of the titles below.

(a) *Officially Dead* – Richard Prescott

You have had a class discussion about the relationship between Mark and Julie in *Officially Dead*. Your teacher has now given you this essay for homework.

In which ways does Mark help Julie?

Write your **essay**.

(b) *Pride and Prejudice* – Jane Austen

You see this notice in your college magazine.

> ### Unpleasant Characters! – Articles wanted.
>
> Have you read a book recently with characters you really disliked? Tell us about them!

Write your **article** about two characters you disliked in *Pride and Prejudice*, giving your reasons.

PAPER 3   USE OF ENGLISH (45 minutes)

Part 1

For questions **1–12**, read the text below and decide which answer (**A, B, C** or **D**) best fits each gap. There is an example at the beginning (**0**).

Mark your answers **on the separate answer sheet**.

Example:

0   **A** planet   **B** world   **C** earth   **D** globe

0	A	B	C	D
	▭	▬	▭	▭

Markets

In practically any country in the **(0)** ..... , you are **(1)** ..... to find a market somewhere. Markets have been with us since **(2)** ..... times, and arose wherever people needed to exchange the goods they produced. For example, a farmer might have exchanged a cow for tools. But just as times have **(3)** ..... , so have market practices. So, **(4)** ..... in early times the main activity **(5)** ..... with markets would have been 'bartering' – in **(6)** ..... words exchanging goods – today most stall-holders wouldn't be too **(7)** ..... on accepting potatoes as payment, for instance, instead of cash.

In contrast, what might be a common **(8)** ..... in a modern market in some countries is a certain amount of 'haggling', where customer and seller eventually **(9)** ..... on a price, after what can sometimes be quite a heated debate. However, behaviour which is **(10)** ..... in a market in one country may not be acceptable in another. Even within one country, there may be some markets where you could haggle quite **(11)** ..... and others where it would be **(12)** ..... not to try!

1 **A** inevitable   **B** confident   **C** definite   **D** sure

2 **A** ancient   **B** antique   **C** old   **D** past

3 **A** changed   **B** turned   **C** developed   **D** differed

4 **A** however   **B** despite   **C** nevertheless   **D** whereas

5 **A** associated   **B** relating   **C** connecting   **D** attached

6 **A** different   **B** other   **C** new   **D** alternative

7 **A** fond   **B** keen   **C** eager   **D** pleased

8 **A** look   **B** vision   **C** sight   **D** view

9 **A** confirm   **B** consent   **C** approve   **D** agree

10 **A** expected   **B** insisted   **C** believed   **D** reckoned

11 **A** simply   **B** plainly   **C** clearly   **D** easily

12 **A** profitable   **B** advisable   **C** noticeable   **D** acceptable

Part 2

For questions **13–24**, read the text below and think of the word which best fits each gap. Use only **one** word in each gap. There is an example at the beginning (**0**).

Write your answers **IN CAPITAL LETTERS on the separate answer sheet**.

Example: | **0** | H | I | S | | | | | | | | | | | | | | | | |

Charles Dickens' childhood experiences

Charles Dickens was one of the greatest nineteenth-century English novelists. At the time of (**0**) ...his... death in 1870 he was a wealthy man, in contrast to the poverty of his early days. His parents (**13**) .... their best to look after him but were always in difficulties (**14**) .... money. Eventually, his father owed (**15**) .... a large amount of money that he was sent to prison for three months.

Two days after his twelfth birthday, Dickens was taken away from school by his parents and made (**16**) .... work in a factory to increase the family income. Factories could be dangerous places in (**17**) .... days and some employers were cruel. Charles was not (**18**) ...even... extremely unhappy, but also ashamed of working there, and he (**19**) .... never forget that period of his life. In his novels Dickens showed just how shocking working and living conditions were.

Working in the factory affected him so deeply that he found (**20**) .... much too painful to speak about in later life. His own wife and children knew (**21**) .... at all about the unhappiness of his childhood while Dickens was still alive, (**22**) .... shortly after his death a biography was published in (**23**) .... Dickens' terrible childhood experiences in the factory were revealed (**24**) .... the first time.

Part 3

For questions **25–34**, read the text below. Use the word given in capitals at the end of some of the lines to form a word that fits in the gap **in the same line**. There is an example at the beginning (**0**).

Write your answers **IN CAPITAL LETTERS on the separate answer sheet**.

Example: | **0** | E | X | T | R | E | M | E | L | Y | | | | | | | | |

The London Underground map

Many people would agree that the London Underground map is

(**0**) ...*extremely*... well designed. It is not only simple and easy to understand   **EXTREME**

but also quite (**25**) .... and, most importantly, it performs its primary   **ATTRACT**

task of guiding both Londoners and (**26**) .... round the Underground   **TOUR**

system in the city very well. The man behind this great (**27**) .... was   **ACHIEVE**

called Henry Beck. He was an (**28**) .... of the London Underground   **EMPLOY**

Drawing Office, and first came up with his design for the map in 1931.

The map which had been in use before 1931 was messy and (**29**) ....   **CLEAR**

Beck decided that a (**30**) .... map, which gives accurate information   **TRADITION**

about distance, was not necessary for the Underground and instead

produced a diagram which showed only the stations on the Underground

system. This new map was an enormous (**31**) .... with the public   **SUCCEED**

when, in 1933, it made its first (**32**) .... on Underground platforms   **APPEAR**

and at station entrances.

The design of the map showed great (**33**) .... because it provided   **ORIGINAL**

a very clear representation of a highly complex network of (**34**) ....   **COMMUNICATE**

Beck's approach was later adopted by most of the world's underground

systems.

Part 4

For questions **35–42**, complete the second sentence so that it has a similar meaning to the first sentence, using the word given. **Do not change the word given.** You must use between **two** and **five** words, including the word given. Here is an example (**0**).

Example:

0 You must do exactly what the manager tells you.

CARRY

You must .... instructions exactly.

The gap can be filled by the words 'carry out the manager's', so you write:

Example: | **0** | *CARRY OUT THE MANAGER'S*

Write **only** the missing words **IN CAPITAL LETTERS on the separate answer sheet**.

---

35 While I was on holiday, a lot of interesting things happened to me.

MY

During .... a lot of interesting experiences.

36 It was careless of you to leave without locking the door.

OUGHT

You .... the door before you left.

37 'Is Pete likely to change his mind?' Rob asked.

CHANCE

'Is there .... changing his mind?' Rob asked.

38 Paul is the only person who has replied to the invitation.

NOBODY

Apart .... replied to the invitation.

39 Are you familiar with his teaching style yet?

USED

Have you .... his teaching style yet?

40 It was such a sunny day that none of us wanted to do any work.

FELT

None of us .... any work because it was such a sunny day.

41 Barbara couldn't sing or dance.

UNABLE

Besides .... , Barbara couldn't dance either.

42 Dinner will be served immediately upon our arrival at the hotel.

SOON

Dinner will be served .... at the hotel.

PAPER 4   LISTENING (approximately 40 minutes)

Part 1

You will hear people talking in eight different situations. For questions **1–8**, choose the best answer (**A**, **B** or **C**).

---

1 You overhear a man talking about an experience he had at an airport.
What did he lose?

    A   his passport

    B   his wallet

    C   a piece of luggage

2 You hear an advertisement on the radio.
What is special about the *Fretlight* guitar?

    A   It plays recorded music.

    B   It teaches you how to play.

    C   It plugs into a computer.

3 You hear part of a radio programme.
What is the presenter talking about?

    A   food safety

    B   meal times

    C   healthy recipes

4 You hear two people discussing a type of pollution.
What do the speakers agree about?

    A   the best way to solve the problem

    B   how they feel about this type of pollution

    C   how they reacted to the solution they saw

5   You hear a conversation between a shop assistant and a customer about a compact disc.
    What was the cause of the problem?

    A   The customer gave the wrong number.

    B   A mistake was made on the order form.

    C   The disc was incorrectly labelled.

6   You overhear a conversation at a football game.
    What does the speaker say about his team?

    A   They're better than usual.

    B   They're as good as he expected.

    C   They tend to be unlucky.

7   You overhear a schoolgirl talking to her friend.
    What does she think about her new teacher?

    A   He is clever.

    B   He is funny.

    C   He is interesting.

8   In a hotel you overhear a conversation.
    Who is the woman?

    A   a tour guide

    B   a tourist

    C   a hotel receptionist

Part 2

You will hear part of a radio interview with a swimming instructor. For questions **9–18**, complete the sentences.

Swimming instructor

Paul works at a hotel in the [_____ **9**_]

He started his job in [_____ **10**_]

He particularly likes meeting [_____ **11**_] there.

Paul isn't interested in teaching [_____ **12**_]

According to Paul, [_____ **13**_] of all adults can't swim.

Paul's students are afraid of going [_____ **14**_]

His students have to put their faces into a salad bowl and

[_____ **15**_] below the surface.

The first thing they do in the pool is to [_____ **16**_]

in the water with their faces down.

Paul thinks it's essential to be [_____ **17**_] in the water.

Most people learn to swim after about [_____ **18**_]

Part 3

You will hear part of a radio programme called *Morning Market*. Five listeners have telephoned the programme because they have something to sell. For questions **19–23**, choose which of the statements (**A–F**) matches the reason each of the people gives for selling their possession. Use the letters only once. There is one extra letter which you do not need to use.

A I didn't enjoy using it.

Speaker 1   **19**

B I made a mistake.

Speaker 2   **20**

C It's an unwanted prize.

Speaker 3   **21**

D It takes up too much space.

Speaker 4   **22**

E I've got something better.

Speaker 5   **23**

F I have health problems.

Part 4

You will hear an interview with a man who makes models for films and television. For questions **24–30**, choose the best answer (**A, B or C**).

24 Matt got a job doing holiday relief work because he wanted

    A   to do part-time work.

    B   a career in photography.

    C   to work in television.

25 What did Matt find 'interesting' about the sixties?

    A   the fascination with space travel

    B   the increased number of comic books

    C   the advances in photography

26 Why were Matt's models used on the news?

    A   They were better than pictures.

    B   Some equipment had been destroyed.

    C   The studio was trying new ideas.

27 Matt thinks he was successful at getting work in television because

    A   he had good experience.

    B   he knew some of the staff.

    C   he was available at the right time.

28 Matt worked on *Bright Star* as

    A   part of a team.

    B   the producer.

    C   a design student.

29 Matt was invited on children's television to

    A   tell stories about his design work.

    B   explain the purpose of space research.

    C   help children make models themselves.

30 Matt remembers *Heart of Darkness* because

    A   it was his favourite comedy.

    B   his work was recognised.

    C   a film was made of it.

PAPER 5   SPEAKING (14 minutes)

You take the Speaking test with another candidate, referred to here as your partner. There are two examiners. One will speak to you and your partner and the other will be listening. Both examiners will award marks.

Part 1 (3 minutes)

The examiner asks you and your partner questions about yourselves. You may be asked about things like 'your home town', 'your interests', 'your career plans', etc.

Part 2 (a one-minute 'long turn' for each candidate, plus 20-second response from the second candidate)

The examiner gives you two photographs and asks you to talk about them for one minute. The examiner then asks your partner a question about your photographs and your partner responds briefly.

Then the examiner gives your partner two different photographs. Your partner talks about these photographs for one minute. This time the examiner asks you a question about your partner's photographs and you respond briefly.

Part 3 (approximately 3 minutes)

The examiner asks you and your partner to talk together. You may be asked to solve a problem or try to come to a decision about something. For example, you might be asked to decide the best way to use some rooms in a language school. The examiner gives you a picture to help you but does not join in the conversation.

Part 4 (approximately 4 minutes)

The interlocutor asks some further questions, which leads to a more general discussion of what you have talked about in Part 3. You may comment on your partner's answers if you wish.

Visual materials for the Speaking test

- How important is it to have a teacher in each situation?

1A

1B

- What difference can these things make to a holiday?
- Which two are the most important?

1E

• What would it be like to live and work in places like these?

1C

1D

- What is difficult about these jobs?

2A

2B

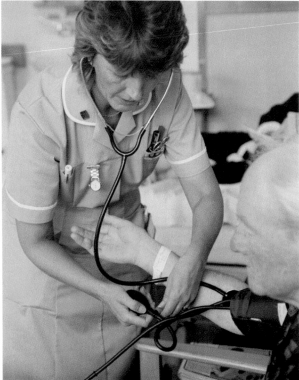

2E

- What are the advantages and disadvantages of the different ways of getting around?
- Which three would be best for seeing as much as possible?

• How important is the telephone to these people?

2C

2D

• How enjoyable would it be to spend an evening in these places?

3A

3B

- How difficult is it to be successful in these professions?
- In which profession is it most difficult to get to the top?

3E

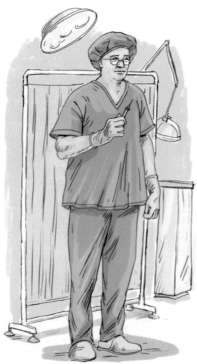

- What will people remember about these occasions?

3C

3D

- What would be exciting about watching these events?

4A

4B

- What are the advantages of having friends?
- In which situation are friends most important?

4E

- What do these pictures show about the different interests of young people?

4C

4D

Test 4

PAPER 1   READING (1 hour)

Part 1

You are going to read an article in which a film critic talks about his work. For questions **1–8**, choose the answer (**A**, **B**, **C** or **D**) which you think fits best according to the text.

Mark your answers **on the separate answer sheet**.

Film Critic

Mark Adams looks back over the last ten years of his work
as a film critic for a newspaper called *The Front Page.*

Writing articles about films for *The Front Page* was my first proper job. Before then I had done bits of reviewing – novels for other newspapers, films for a magazine and anything I was asked to do for the radio. That was how I met Tom Seaton, the first arts editor of *The Front Page*, who had also written for radio and television. He hired me, but Tom was not primarily a journalist, or he would certainly have been more careful in choosing his staff.

At first, his idea was that a team of critics should take care of the art forms that didn't require specialised knowledge: books, TV, theatre, film and radio. There would be a weekly lunch at which we would make our choices from the artistic material that Tom had decided we should cover, though there would also be guests to make the atmosphere sociable.

It all felt like a bit of a dream at that time: a new newspaper, and I was one of the team. It seemed so unlikely that a paper could be introduced into a crowded market. It seemed just as likely that a millionaire wanted to help me personally, and was pretending to employ me. Such was my lack of self-confidence. In fact, the first time I saw someone reading the newspaper on the London Underground, then turning to a page on which one of my reviews appeared, I didn't know where to look.

line 31   Tom's original scheme for a team of critics for the arts never took off. It was a good idea, but we didn't get together as planned and so everything was done by phone. It turned out, too, that the general public out there preferred to associate a reviewer with a single subject area, and so I chose film. Without Tom's initial push, though, we would hardly have come up with the present arrangement, by which I write an extended weekly piece, usually on one film.

The luxury of this way of working suits me well. I wouldn't have been interested in the more standard film critic's role, which involves considering every film that comes out. That's a routine that would make me stale in no time at all. I would soon be sinking into my seat on a Monday morning with the sigh, 'What insulting rubbish must I sit through now?' – a style of sigh that can often be heard in screening rooms around the world.

The space I am given allows me to broaden my argument – or forces me, in an uninteresting week, to make something out of nothing. But what is my role in the public arena? I assume that people choose what films to go to on the basis of the stars, the publicity or the director. There is also such a thing as loyalty to 'type' or its opposite. It can only rarely happen that someone who hates westerns buys a ticket for one after reading a review, or a love story addict avoids a romantic film because of what the papers say.

So if a film review isn't really a consumer guide, what is it? I certainly don't feel I have a responsibility to be 'right' about a movie. Nor do I think there should be a certain number of 'great' and 'bad' films each year. All I have to do is put forward an argument. I'm not a judge, and nor would I want to be.

1 What do we learn about Tom Seaton in the first paragraph?

    A He encouraged Mark to become a writer.
    B He has worked in various areas of the media.
    C He met Mark when working for television.
    D He prefers to employ people that he knows.

2 The weekly lunches were planned in order to

    A help the writers get to know each other.
    B provide an informal information session.
    C distribute the work that had to be done.
    D entertain important visitors from the arts.

3 When Mark first started working for *The Front Page*, he

    A doubted the paper would succeed.
    B was embarrassed at being recognised.
    C felt it needed some improvement.
    D was surprised to be earning so much.

4 What does Mark mean when he says that Tom's scheme 'never took off' (line 31)?

    A It was unpopular.
    B It wasted too much time.
    C It wasn't planned properly.
    D It wasn't put into practice.

5 In the end, the organisation of the team was influenced by

    A readers' opinions.
    B the availability of writers.
    C pressure of time.
    D the popularity of subjects.

6 Why does Mark refer to his way of working as a 'luxury' (line 40)?

    A He can please more readers.
    B He is able to make choices.
    C His working hours are flexible.
    D He is able to see a lot of films.

7 In Mark's opinion, his articles

    A are seldom read by filmgoers.
    B are ignored by stars and film directors.
    C have little effect on public viewing habits.
    D are more persuasive than people realise.

8 Which of the following best describes what Mark says about his work?

    A His success varies from year to year.
    B He prefers to write about films he likes.
    C He can freely express his opinion.
    D He writes according to accepted rules.

Part 2

You are going to read a newspaper article about a dentist. Seven sentences have been removed from the article. Choose from the sentences **A–H** the one which fits each gap (**9–15**). There is one extra sentence which you do not need to use.

Mark your answers **on the separate answer sheet**.

Fun at the Dentist's?

If you walk into W. Lloyd Jerome's dental surgery in the centre of Glasgow, you'll see bright modern paintings on the wall and a fashionable blue couch which patients sit on while he checks their teeth. Jerome says, 'Fifty per cent of the population only go to the dentist when they're in pain rather than attending for regular check-ups. That's because they're frightened.'

To counteract this, he has tried to create an environment where people are not afraid. ' **9** ' I find that's one of the things that people associate with pain. In fact, my philosophy is that dental treatment should take place in an atmosphere of relaxation, interest and above all enjoyment.'

Which is all highly shocking for anyone (most of us in fact) who has learnt to associate dental treatment with pain, or at the very least, with formal, clinical visits. Jerome says, ' **10** '

Virtual-reality headsets are one of his new relaxation techniques. ' **11** ' The headsets are used for the initial check-up, where the patient sits comfortably on the blue couch and watches a film about underwater wildlife while I look at their teeth. Then the headset switches to a special camera, to give the patient a visual tour around their mouth.' Surprisingly, most patients seem to enjoy this part of their visit to the dentist.

Another key point is that the surgery smells more like a perfume shop than a dentist's. Today there is the smell of orange. Jerome explains, ' **12** ' Smell is very important. That dental smell of surgical spirit can get the heart racing in minutes if you're frightened of dentists.' I certainly found the delicate smell in the surgery very pleasant.

Although he is known as Glasgow's most fashionable dentist, Jerome is keen to point out that he takes his work very seriously. ' **13** '

For example, Jerome uses a special instrument which sprays warm water on the teeth to clean them, rather than scraping them. ' **14** '

Five years ago, Jerome went to the United States to do research into dental techniques. ' **15** ', he explains. He sees his patient-centred attitude as the start of a gradual movement towards less formality in the conservative British dentistry profession.

At that moment, a patient arrives. Jerome rushes over, offers him a cup of tea (herbal or regular), asks him what video he'd like to watch and leads him gently towards the chair. The patient seems to be enjoying this five-star treatment and no wonder. The surgery seems more like an elegant beauty parlour than a mainstream dental practice.

A One of the things I found out there was that when you make it easier for the patient you make it easier for yourself.

B That's why I took the decision not to wear a white coat.

C If people are relaxed, entertained and correctly treated, they will forget such previous negative experiences.

D The relaxation techniques are important but the quality of the treatment is of course the most important thing.

E We were the first practice in Britain to introduce them and they're proving very popular.

F It feels a bit strange at first, but as long as people are relaxed, it's not painful at all.

G Now I'm sure that they actually look forward to their visits here.

H When people walk in, I want them to realise with all their senses that it's not like going to the dentist's.

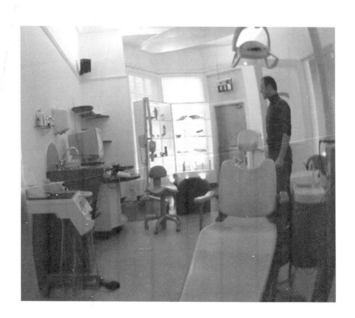

Part 3

You are going to read a magazine article about theme parks in Britain. For questions **16–30**, choose from the theme parks (**A–E**). The theme parks may be chosen more than once.

Mark your answers **on the separate answer sheet.**

Of which theme parks are the following stated?

We had no previous experience of places like this.	**16**
Some of the children showed they were frightened on a certain ride.	**17**
The children were all young enough to enjoy it.	**18**
It was good that you could find somewhere to rest.	**19**
It was more enjoyable than we had expected.	**20**
The children disagreed about what was the most frightening ride.	**21**
The surroundings are not particularly attractive.	**22**
We didn't mind having to wait to go on the rides.	**23**
The children wanted to stay longer than we did.	**24**
One of the rides seemed to finish very quickly.	**25**
We were glad that the children couldn't go on a certain ride.	**26**
One of the children had a better time than we had expected.	**27**
It makes a claim which is accurate.	**28**
None of the rides would frighten young children very much.	**29**
The manner of some employees seemed rather unfriendly.	**30**

Variations on a Theme

If you're thinking of taking children to a theme park, there are dozens to choose from in Britain. We asked five families to test the best.

A Fun Island – The Burns family

Last year we went to a huge theme park in the US and we thought that Fun Island might seem dull by comparison. In fact, we were impressed. The park tries hard to cater for younger children, so our three-year-old didn't feel left out. The kids all loved the Crocodile Ride and the Giant Wheel. There's a special dodgems ride for the very young kids, which was a great success. For older children, there are scarier rides, such as Splash Out, where you end up jumping in a pool! After five hours, Steve and I were ready to call it a day, but the children objected because they were having such fun. Our only criticism would be that the park is slightly lacking in atmosphere, and the scenery leaves something to be desired. But the staff are extremely helpful and we felt it was clean, well organised and very security-conscious.

B Wonderland – The McMillan family

None of us had been to a theme park before, so we didn't know what to expect. We thought Oscar might be too young, but he adored it. He was in heaven on the Mountain Train, and particularly liked Little Land, with its small replicas of famous buildings that were at his level! The older children enjoyed the ferris wheel, and loved driving the toy cars on a proper road layout. We spent six hours there and were glad that there were places where you could put your feet up. The landscaping is perfect and the staff very helpful and friendly. And there's something for everyone, adults included.

C Adventure World – The Jeffree family

After seven hours we felt there was still a lot to see. The children loved the Big Top Circus, which had a fantastic trapeze act and kept us on the edge of our seats. We went on the Terror Line and, although the girls were rather scared and kept their eyes shut most of the time, they said they'd enjoyed it. Their favourite ride was Running River, where you think you're going to get soaked, but you don't. For younger children, Toy Land is great fun. The children had a look at the new ride, Fear

Factor, but we breathed a sigh of relief when they found that they were too small to go on it! The park is so well designed that even queuing for rides isn't too boring. It's spotlessly clean, and the staff are great. On one ride I couldn't sit with both girls, so a member of staff offered to go with one of them.

D The Great Park – The Langridge family

We arrived at one o'clock and were disappointed that the park was only open until 5 p.m. This is a super theme park for younger children because the rides aren't too terrifying. I'm a real coward but even I enjoyed myself. We all adored Exotic Travels, a boat ride which starts off quite tamely and then becomes terrific fun. We queued for half an hour for Lightning River, and then it was over before we knew it! I wouldn't go on the Big Leap, but if you have the nerve, it looked great. If the children had been a little older, they might have found it a bit tame, but they were all in the right age group and they loved it.

E Fantasy World – The Breakall family

According to the park's advertising there is 'No Limit to the Fun', and we certainly felt that was true. Europe's tallest roller-coaster, the Rocket, dominates the skyline, and Ben thought it was the most terrifying of the rides, although Jennie said the Hanger, where you hang upside-down 30 metres above the ground, was even worse! There are a dozen or so main rides, which the older children went on several times. Sarah was too small for a couple of them, but enjoyed the Long Slide. We found the staff attitudes were mixed. Some of them were great with the younger children, but the welcome wasn't always as warm. You need a full day to enjoy Fantasy World. We wouldn't have dared tell the kids we were going home early.

PAPER 2   WRITING (1 hour 20 minutes)

Part 1

You **must** answer this question. Write your answer in **120–150** words in an appropriate style.

1   You have received this letter from your English-speaking friend, Alex. Read the letter and the notes you have made. Then write a letter to Alex, using **all** your notes.

> *You won't believe this – I wrote an article for a travel magazine and I've won first prize in the competition! The prize is a ten-day holiday in Scotland for two people. Would you like to come with me?* — Yes, fantastic!
>
> *We could either go in June or July. Which would be better for you?*
>
> Say which and why
>
> *The prize includes tickets for either the theatre or a sports event. Which would you prefer?* — Tell Alex
>
> *At the end of the trip we have to write an article about the holiday for the travel magazine, but we need to plan it in advance. I'd like to write about the tourist sites. Would you be happy to write about the food?*
>
> No, suggest . . .
>
> *Write back soon!*
>
> *Alex*

Write your **letter**. You must use grammatically correct sentences with accurate spelling and punctuation in a style appropriate for the situation.

Do not write any postal addresses.

Part 2

Write an answer to **one** of the questions **2–5** in this part. Write your answer in **120–180** words in an appropriate style.

---

2   After a class discussion on the media's treatment of famous people, your teacher has asked you to write an essay, giving your opinions on the following statement:

   Famous people, such as politicians and film stars, deserve to have a private life without journalists following them all the time.

   Write your **essay**.

3   You see this announcement in an international magazine.

   > We invite you, our readers, to write an article on:
   > ### The Home of the Future
   > In what ways do you think people's homes will be
   > different in the future?
   > In what ways will they still be the same?
   > The writer of the best article will win a prize.

   Write your **article**.

4   Your English teacher has asked you to write a story for the college magazine. Your story must **begin** with the following words:

   It was dangerous, but I knew I had to do it.

   Write your **story**.

5   Answer **one** of the following two questions based on **one** of the titles below.

   (a) *Officially Dead* – Richard Prescott

   You have had a class discussion about what happens to Julie in *Officially Dead*. Now your English teacher has given you this essay for homework.

   How does Julie's life change after her husband's death?

   Write your **essay**.

   (b) *Pride and Prejudice* – Jane Austen

   You have received this letter from your English friend, Kate.

   > I've recently read the book and seen the film of *Pride and Prejudice*.
   > It's a very old-fashioned story – why do you think it is still so popular
   > with people today?
   > Write soon, Kate

   Write your **letter**.

PAPER 3   USE OF ENGLISH (45 minutes)

Part 1

For questions **1–12**, read the text below and decide which answer (**A, B, C** or **D**) best fits each gap. There is an example at the beginning (**0**).

Mark your answers **on the separate answer sheet**.

Example:

0   **A** recommended   **B** reminded   **C** recognised   **D** remembered

0	A	B	C	D
	—	—	—	▬

Famous explorer

Captain James Cook is (**0**) ..... today for being one of Britain's most famous explorers of the 18th century. Cook was (**1**) ..... most other explorers of the same period as he did not come from a wealthy family and had to work hard to (**2**) ..... his position in life. He was lucky to be (**3**) ..... by his father's employer, who saw that he was a bright boy and paid for him to attend the village school. At sixteen, he started (**4**) ..... in a shop in a fishing village, and this was a turning (**5**) ..... in his life. He developed an interest in the sea and eventually joined the Royal Navy in order to see more of the world.

Cook was (**6**) ..... by sailing, astronomy and the production of maps, and quickly became an expert in these subjects. He was also one of the first people to (**7**) ..... that scurvy, an illness often suffered by sailors, could be prevented by careful (**8**) ..... to diet. It was during his (**9**) ..... to the Pacific Ocean that Cook made his historic landing in Australia and the (**10**) ..... discovery that New Zealand was two (**11**) ..... islands. He became a national hero and still (**12**) ..... one today.

1 **A** different   **B** contrary   **C** distinct   **D** unlike

2 **A** manage   **B** succeed   **C** achieve   **D** fulfil

3 **A** remarked   **B** viewed   **C** glanced   **D** noticed

4 **A** trade   **B** work   **C** career   **D** job

5 **A** moment   **B** instant   **C** point   **D** mark

6 **A** keen   **B** eager   **C** fascinated   **D** enthusiastic

7 **A** regard   **B** estimate   **C** catch   **D** realise

8 **A** attention   **B** organisation   **C** observation   **D** selection

9 **A** travel   **B** voyage   **C** excursion   **D** tour

10 **A** serious   **B** superior   **C** major   **D** leading

11 **A** shared   **B** particular   **C** common   **D** separate

12 **A** remains   **B** stands   **C** maintains   **D** keeps

Part 2

For questions **13–24**, read the text below and think of the word which best fits each gap. Use only **one** word in each gap. There is an example at the beginning (**0**).

Write your answers **IN CAPITAL LETTERS on the separate answer sheet**.

Example: | 0 | M | O | S | T | | | | | | | | | | | | | | |

The Inferno ski race

The Inferno is the oldest and (**0**) ...*most*... celebrated of all amateur ski races. It is held every January, near Mürren in Switzerland. Anyone can take part, as (**13**) .... as they belong to a ski racing club.

The Inferno was the invention of a British businessman called Henry Lunn, who came up (**14**) .... the idea of the package holiday in the early 1900s and began taking groups of people to the Alps for winter sports. Henry's son, Arnold, grew very fond (**15**) .... Mürren and he founded a ski club there in 1924. Four years (**16**) .... , seventeen of the club's members took part (**17**) .... the first Inferno race, from the top of the 2,970 metre Schilthorn mountain to Mürren below.

In those early days, they (**18**) .... to climb for six hours from the railway station in Mürren (**19**) .... the start of the race. Today, racers use a cable car which (**20**) .... about twenty minutes. In the first race, the winning time for the fourteen-kilometre race was one hour, twelve minutes. (**21**) .... days it tends to be almost exactly an hour less. Although the skiers are very (**22**) .... faster now, some things haven't changed. The course, (**23**) .... is steep and has sharp bends, remains (**24**) .... of the most demanding and frightening in the world.

Part 3

For questions **25–34**, read the text below. Use the word given in capitals at the end of some of the lines to form a word that fits in the gap **in the same line**. There is an example at the beginning (**0**).

Write your answers **IN CAPITAL LETTERS on the separate answer sheet**.

Example:

| 0 | S | H | O | R | T | L | Y | | | | | | | | | |

Running round the world

Clive Baker will (**0**) ...*shortly*... be setting off on a 50,000 km run, hoping   **SHORT**

to add his name to the very small and select list of people who have

performed the (**25**) .... act of running all the way round the world.   **ORDINARY**

On the run he will experience extremes of temperature, from the

(**26**) .... Russian winter to the burning African summer. As if that is   **FREEZE**

not bad enough, he has no back-up team for (**27**) .... and will be   **ASSIST**

running alone, carrying all his (**28**) .... on his back.   **EQUIP**

When interviewed, however, Mr Baker suggested the real problem

would lie elsewhere. 'My biggest fear is not the physical challenge,

but (**29**) .... ,' Mr Baker said. 'I'm as sociable as anyone and I'm very   **LONELY**

(**30**) .... that, despite the difficulties that lie ahead, I will still be able   **HOPE**

to form many (**31**) .... on the way.'   **FRIEND**

On a trial of 2,000 km, run under the blazing (**32**) .... of the African sun,   **HOT**

he came across wild baboons and (**33**) .... snakes, but such dangers   **POISON**

have not put him off. His trial run proved that a target of 60 kilometres

a day was (**34**) .... 'I have made up my mind to do it and I will.   **REASON**

Running is my life,' he said.

Part 4

For questions **35–42**, complete the second sentence so that it has a similar meaning to the first sentence, using the word given. **Do not change the word given**. You must use between **two** and **five** words, including the word given. Here is an example (**0**).

Example:

0 You must do exactly what the manager tells you.

CARRY

You must .... instructions exactly.

The gap can be filled by the words 'carry out the manager's' so you write:

Example:

0	*CARRY OUT THE MANAGER'S*

Write **only** the missing words **IN CAPITAL LETTERS on the separate answer sheet**.

---

35 That's the strangest film I've ever seen!

STRANGE

I've .... film before!

36 A very friendly taxi driver drove us into town.

DRIVEN

We .... a very friendly taxi driver.

37 My aunt was determined to pay for our tickets.

INSISTED

My aunt .... for our tickets.

38 The manager failed to persuade Karen to take the job.

SUCCEED

The manager .... Karen to take the job.

39 'I'd rather you didn't use that mobile phone in here,' said the librarian.

   MIND

   'Would .... that mobile phone in here?' said the librarian.

40 John impressed his new boss by settling down to work quickly.

   GOOD

   John .... his new boss by settling down to work quickly.

41 Tony regrets lying to his teacher.

   WISHES

   Tony .... his teacher the truth.

42 I found it difficult to follow the instructions.

   TROUBLE

   I .... the instructions.

PAPER 4   LISTENING (approximately 40 minutes)

Part 1

You will hear people talking in eight different situations. For questions **1–8**, choose the best answer (**A**, **B** or **C**).

---

1   You overhear some people talking at a party in a hotel.
Where did the people first meet each other?

  A   at school

  B   at work

  C   at a wedding

2   You overhear a conversation in a restaurant.
Why haven't they seen each other lately?

  A   He has been too busy.

  B   He has been ill.

  C   He has been away.

3   You overhear someone talking about a concert.
How did she feel at the time?

  A   angry

  B   frightened

  C   disappointed

4   You hear a writer of children's stories talking about books and compact discs.
What advantage does he think books have over compact discs?

  A   They may last for a longer time.

  B   They are easier to look after.

  C   They contain better quality material.

5 You hear a husband and wife talking about their summer holidays.
   What problem do they have?

   A They really hate flying anywhere.

   B They can never think of anywhere to go.

   C They never agree about what to do.

6 You hear a researcher being asked about her work.
   What is she doing when she speaks?

   A denying an accusation

   B disproving a theory

   C accepting a criticism

7 You overhear a woman talking to a friend on a train.
   What does the woman think of the course she has attended?

   A It has made her feel more confident.

   B It has made her feel less confident.

   C It hasn't made much difference to how she feels.

8 You overhear a woman speaking on the radio.
   What is she doing?

   A complaining about something

   B apologising for something

   C explaining something

Part 2

You will hear a radio report about dolphins. For questions **9–18**, complete the sentences.

 **Dolphins**

Dolphins have been known to protect swimmers from sharks by getting into a

	9

Dolphins and humans have | | **10** | of the same size.

Swimming with dolphins can help common problems like

	11

Some people think dolphins are able to recognise human | | **12** |

Dolphins have been used to teach children to | | **13** |

Swimming with dolphins is used as a | | **14** |

in projects with children.

In one jaw, dolphins have as many as | | **15** |

Dolphins can maintain a fast pace in the water for | | **16** |

without stopping.

Dolphins make use of | | **17** | to find fish.

Dolphins can be caught in | | **18** | or damaged by pollution.

Part 3

You will hear five different people talking about the head teacher or principal of their former secondary school. For questions **19–23**, choose from the list (**A–F**) what each speaker is saying. Use the letters only once. There is one extra letter which you do not need to use.

A She favoured the talented students.

| | Speaker 1 | | 19 |

B She prepared us for the real world.

| | Speaker 2 | | 20 |

C She encouraged us to be imaginative.

| | Speaker 3 | | 21 |

D She was ahead of her time.

| | Speaker 4 | | 22 |

E She was concerned about the environment.

| | Speaker 5 | | 23 |

F She encouraged competitiveness.

Part 4

You will hear an interview with a tour leader who works for an adventure company in Africa. For questions **24–30**, choose the best answer (**A**, **B** or **C**).

24 Don says that most of his passengers

  A are not students.

  B are looking for jobs.

  C work in conservation.

25 When Don first meets a group, he

  A gives them blankets for the overnight trip.

  B shows them where to sit on the truck.

  C checks they have the right equipment.

26 Don remembers one trip when

  A he failed to take enough food.

  B someone made a mistake with the food.

  C someone complained about the food.

27 Don oversees the domestic work because

  A he doesn't like to lose things.

  B it has to be done within an hour.

  C people complain if things are dirty.

28 If people argue, Don says that he

  A prefers not to get involved.

  B separates the people concerned.

  C asks the group for a solution.

29 Don says that he sometimes

    A   needs to get to sleep early.

    B   has to camp in a noisy area.

    C   tells people when to go to bed.

30 What does Don say about getting up?

    A   He ignores any complaints about the time.

    B   He varies his schedule according to the group.

    C   He forces everyone to be quick about it.

PAPER 5   SPEAKING (14 minutes)

You take the Speaking test with another candidate, referred to here as your partner.
There are two examiners. One will speak to you and your partner and the other will be
listening. Both examiners will award marks.

Part 1 (3 minutes)

The examiner asks you and your partner questions about yourselves. You may be asked
about things like 'your home town', 'your interests', 'your career plans', etc.

Part 2 (a one-minute 'long turn' for each candidate, plus 20-second response from the second candidate)

The examiner gives you two photographs and asks you to talk about them for one
minute. The examiner then asks your partner a question about your photographs and
your partner responds briefly.

Then the examiner gives your partner two different photographs. Your partner talks
about these photographs for one minute. This time the examiner asks you a question
about your partner's photographs and you respond briefly.

Part 3 (approximately 3 minutes)

The examiner asks you and your partner to talk together. You may be asked to solve a
problem or try to come to a decision about something. For example, you might be asked
to decide the best way to use some rooms in a language school. The examiner gives
you a picture to help you but does not join in the conversation.

Part 4 (approximately 4 minutes)

The interlocutor asks some further questions, which leads to a more general discussion
of what you have talked about in Part 3. You may comment on your partner's answers
if you wish.

Paper 5 frames

Test 1

Note: In the examination, there will be both an assessor and an interlocutor in the room.
The visual material for **Test 1** appears on pages C1 and C4 (Part 2), and C2–C3 (Part 3).

Part 1   3 minutes (5 minutes for groups of three)

Interlocutor: Good morning/afternoon/evening. My name is .... and this is my
                     colleague ....
                     And your names are?
                     Can I have your mark sheets, please?
                     Thank you.
                     First of all, we'd like to know something about you.

- Where are you from *(Candidate A)*?
- And you *(Candidate B)*?
- What do you like about living *(here / name of candidate's home town)*?
- And what about you *(Candidate A/B)*?

Select one or more questions from any of the following categories, as appropriate.

Personal experience

- Do you enjoy buying presents for people? ..... (Is it ever difficult to buy for someone?)
- What was the best present you received recently? ..... (Who gave it to you?)

Daily life

- Is your weekday routine different from your weekend routine? ..... (In what ways?)
- What do you look forward to at the end of the day?

Media

- How much TV do you watch? ..... (What kind of programmes do you *not* enjoy?)
- Do you buy magazines or newspapers regularly? ..... (Why? / Why not?)

Part 2   4 minutes (6 minutes for groups of three)

Teachers and children
Places

Interlocutor:	In this part of the test, I'm going to give each of you two photographs. I'd like you to talk about your photographs on your own for about a minute, and also to answer a short question about your partner's photographs.
	(Candidate A), it's your turn first. Here are your photographs. They show teachers and children.
	Indicate pictures 1A and 1B on page C1 to Candidate A.
	I'd like you to compare the photographs, and say how important it is to have a teacher in each situation. All right?
Candidate A:	[*1 minute*]
Interlocutor:	Thank you.
	(Candidate B), would you like to teach children?
Candidate B:	[*Approximately 20 seconds*]
Interlocutor:	Thank you.
	Now, *(Candidate B)*, here are your two photographs. They show places where people live.
	Indicate pictures 1C and 1D on page C4 to Candidate B.
	I'd like you to compare the photographs, and say what you think it would be like to live and work in places like these. All right?
Candidate B:	[*1 minute*]
Interlocutor:	Thank you.
	(Candidate A), where would you prefer to live?
Candidate A:	[*Approximately 20 seconds*]
Interlocutor:	Thank you.

Parts 3 and 4   7 minutes (9 minutes for groups of three)

A holiday

Part 3

Interlocutor: Now, I'd like you to talk about something together for about three minutes. *(4 minutes for groups of three)*

Here are some pictures which show things that can make a difference to a holiday.

Indicate the set of pictures 1E on pages C2–C3 to the candidates.

First, talk to each other about the differences these things can make to a holiday. Then decide which two are the most important. All right?

Candidates: [*3 minutes, 4 minutes for groups of three*]

Interlocutor: Thank you.

Part 4

Interlocutor: *Select any of the following questions, as appropriate:*

- Why do you think we need holidays?
- Do you prefer to plan your holiday or to go at the last minute?
  ..... (Why? / Why not?)

> *Select any of the following prompts as appropriate:*
> - What do you think?
> - Do you agree?
> - And you?

- How important is it to experience something new when you go on holiday?
- What would you find enjoyable about a holiday in a large city?
- How does the weather affect holidays in your country?
- How well do you know the area where you're living now?

Thank you. That is the end of the test.

Test 2

Note: In the examination, there will be both an assessor and an interlocutor in the room.
The visual material for **Test 2** appears on pages C5 and C8 (Part 2), and C6–C7 (Part 3).

Part 1   3 minutes (5 minutes for groups of three)

Interlocutor:	Good morning/afternoon/evening. My name is .... and this is my colleague ....

And your names are?
Can I have your mark sheets, please?
Thank you.
First of all, we'd like to know something about you.

- Where are you from *(Candidate A)*?
- And you *(Candidate B)*?
- What do you like about living *(here / name of candidate's home town)*?
- And what about you *(Candidate A/B)*?

Select one or more questions from any of the following categories, as appropriate.

Free time

- Are you an active person in your free time? ..... (What sort of things do you do?)
- When did you last play a sport? ..... (What was it?)

Travel

- Which country would you most like to visit? ..... (Why?)
- Do you prefer going on holiday in a small group or a large group? ..... (Why?)

Personal experience

- What is your favourite time of year? ..... (Why?)
- Do you think you will always have the same friends? ..... (Why? / Why not?)

Part 2   4 minutes (6 minutes for groups of three)

Jobs
Using the telephone

Interlocutor: In this part of the test, I'm going to give each of you two photographs. I'd like you to talk about your photographs on your own for about a minute, and also to answer a short question about your partner's photographs.

(Candidate A), it's your turn first. Here are your photographs. They show people doing different jobs.

Indicate pictures 2A and 2B on page C5 to Candidate A.

I'd like you to compare the photographs, and say what you think is difficult about these jobs. All right?

Candidate A:	[*1 minute*]
Interlocutor:	Thank you.

(*Candidate B*), would you like to do either of these jobs?

Candidate B:	[*Approximately 20 seconds*]
Interlocutor:	Thank you.

Now, (*Candidate B*), here are your two photographs. They show people using the telephone.

Indicate pictures 2C and 2D on page C8 to Candidate B.

I'd like you to compare the photographs, and say how important you think the telephone is to these people. All right?

Candidate B:	[*1 minute*]
Interlocutor:	Thank you. (*Candidate A*), do you use the telephone a lot?
Candidate A:	[*Approximately 20 seconds*]
Interlocutor:	Thank you.

Parts 3 and 4   7 minutes (9 minutes for groups of three)

Part 3

Island holiday resort

Interlocutor:	Now, I'd like you to talk about something together for about three minutes. (*4 minutes for groups of three*)

Here is a picture of an island holiday resort and some ways of getting around.

Indicate the set of pictures 2E on pages C6–C7 to the candidates.

First, talk to each other about the advantages and disadvantages of the different ways of getting around. Then decide which three would be best for seeing as much of the island as possible. All right?

Candidates:	[*3 minutes (4 minutes for groups of three)*]
Interlocutor:	Thank you.

Part 4

Interlocutor: *Select any of the following questions, as*
                  appropriate.

Select any of the following prompts as appropriate:

- Would you choose to go to a small island for a holiday? ..... (Why? / Why not?)
- Do you think there should be a limit on the number of tourists who go to islands like this one? ..... (Why? / Why not?)

Prompts:
- What do you think?
- Do you agree?
- And you?

- How active do you like to be on holiday?
- Do you think it's important for people to travel? ..... (Why? / Why not?)
- What's the worst holiday you've ever had?
- Are there unusual holidays in your country? ..... (Tell us about one.)

Thank you. That is the end of the test.

Test 3

Note: In the examination, there will be both an assessor and an interlocutor in the room
The visual material for **Test 3** appears on pages C9 and C12 (Part 2), and C10–C11 (Part 3).

Part 1   3 minutes (5 minutes for groups of three)

Interlocutor: Good morning/afternoon/evening. My name is ………… and this is my
colleague ………… .
And your names are?
Can I have your mark sheets, please?
Thank you.
First of all, we'd like to know something about you.

- Where are you from *(Candidate A)*?
- And you *(Candidate B)*?
- What do you like about living *(here / name of candidate's home town)*?
- And what about you *(Candidate A/B)*?

Select one or more questions from any of the following categories, as appropriate.

Leisure time

- Do you spend most of your free time on your own or with friends? ….. (What do you usually do?)
- Do you prefer to be outside or inside when you have free time? ….. (Why?)

Likes and dislikes

- What is your favourite part of the day? ….. (Why?)
- Do you enjoy shopping? ….. (What sort of things do you *not* enjoy buying?)

Science and technology

- How much do you use the Internet? ….. (What do you use it for?)
- Do you enjoy playing computer games? ….. (Why? / Why not?)

Part 2   4 minutes (6 minutes for groups of three)

Places in the evening
Special occasions

Interlocutor: In this part of the test, I'm going to give each of you two photographs. I'd
like you to talk about your photographs on your own for about a minute,
and also to answer a short question about your partner's photographs.

(Candidate A), it's your turn first. Here are your photographs. They show
different places in the evening.

Indicate pictures 3A and 3B on page C9 to Candidate A.

I'd like you to compare the photographs, and say how enjoyable you think it would be to spend an evening in these places. All right?

Candidate A:	[*1 minute*]
Interlocutor:	Thank you.

(Candidate B), which place would you prefer to spend an evening in?

Candidate B:	[*Approximately 20 seconds*]
Interlocutor:	Thank you.

Now, *(Candidate B)*, here are your two photographs. They show different special occasions.

Indicate pictures 3C and 3D on page C12 to Candidate B.

I'd like you to compare the photographs, and say what you think the people will remember about these occasions. All right?

Candidate B:	[*1 minute*]
Interlocutor:	Thank you.

(Candidate A), do you enjoy special occasions?

Candidate A:	[*Approximately 20 seconds*]
Interlocutor:	Thank you.

Parts 3 and 4   7 minutes (9 minutes for groups of three)

Part 3

At the top

Interlocutor:	Now, I'd like you to talk about something together for about three minutes. *(4 minutes for groups of three)*

Here are some pictures of people who are at the top of their professions.

Indicate the set of pictures 3E on pages C10–C11 to the candidates.

First, talk to each other about how difficult it is to be successful in these professions. Then decide in which profession it is most difficult to get to the top. All right?

Candidates:	[*3 minutes (4 minutes for groups of three)*]
Interlocutor:	Thank you.

Part 4

Interlocutor: *Select any of the following questions as appropriate:*

Select any of the following prompts as appropriate:

- *What do you think?*
- *Do you agree?*
- *And you?*

- What are the advantages of being famous?
- Which famous person do you most admire? ..... (Why?)
- How important is luck if you want to be successful?
- How important is it for people to have dreams and ambitions?
- Some people become famous when they are very young. What problems do you think this might cause?
- As well as being successful at work, what other things in life make people happy?

Thank you. That is the end of the test.

Test 4

Note: In the examination, there will be both an assessor and an interlocutor in the room.
The visual material for **Test 4** appears on pages C13 and C16 (Part 2) and C14–C15 (Part 3).

Part 1   3 minutes (5 minutes for groups of three)

Interlocutor: Good morning/afternoon/evening. My name is .... and this is my
colleague ....
And your names are?
Can I have your mark sheets, please?
Thank you.
First of all, we'd like to know something about you.

- Where are you from *(Candidate A)*?
- And you *(Candidate B)*?
- What do you like about living *(here / name of candidate's home town)*?
- And what about you *(Candidate A/B)*?

Select one or more questions from any of the following categories, as appropriate.

Likes and dislikes

- What kind of music do you listen to? ..... (When do you listen to music?)
- Do you enjoy watching films? ..... (Tell us about a film you've enjoyed recently.)

Work and education

- Do you think you will use English a lot in the future? ..... (In what ways?)
- What other languages would you like to learn? ..... (Why?)

Travel and holidays

- What is your favourite place for a holiday? ..... (Why?)
- What do you enjoy doing on holiday?

Part 2   4 minutes (6 minutes for groups of three)

Public events
Young people

Interlocutor: In this part of the test, I'm going to give each of you two photographs. I'd
like you to talk about your photographs on your own for about a minute,
and also to answer a short question about your partner's photographs.

(Candidate A), it's your turn first. Here are your photographs. They show
different public events.

Indicate pictures 4A and 4B on page C13 to Candidate A.

I'd like you to compare the photographs, and say what you think would be exciting about watching these events. All right?

Candidate A: [*1 minute*]

Interlocutor: Thank you.

                 (Candidate B), do you like watching public events?

Candidate B: [*Approximately 20 seconds*]

Interlocutor: Thank you.

                 Now, *(Candidate B)*, here are your two photographs. They show young people at home.

                 Indicate pictures 4C and 4D on page C16 to Candidate B.

                 I'd like you to compare the photographs, and say what they show about the different interests of the young people. All right?

Candidate B: [*1 minute*]

Interlocutor: Thank you.

                 (Candidate A), are you interested in football?

Candidate A: [*Approximately 20 seconds*]

Interlocutor: Thank you.

Parts 3 and 4   7 minutes (9 minutes for groups of three)

Part 3

Friends

Interlocutor: Now, I'd like you to talk about something together for about three minutes. *(4 minutes for groups of three)*

                 Here are some pictures suggesting what friends are for.

                 Indicate the set of pictures 4E on pages C14–C15 to the candidates.

                 First, talk to each other about the advantages of having friends in situations like these. Then decide in which situation friends are most important. All right?

Candidates: [*3 minutes (4 minutes for groups of three)*]

Interlocutor: Thank you.

Part 4

Interlocutor: *Select any of the following questions, as*
                  appropriate:

| | *Select any of the following* |
| | *prompts as appropriate:* |

- Are friends more important than family?
  ..... (Why? / Why not?)
- What are the advantages of having friends
  older or younger than you?
- What sort of problems can having friends cause?
- What is the difference between a friend and a best friend?
- How do relationships change as people get older?
- How does your behaviour change when you're with people you don't
  know?

Select any of the following prompts as appropriate:

- What do you think?
- Do you agree?
- And you?

Thank you. That is the end of the test.

Marks and results

Paper 1   Reading

Candidates record their answers on a separate answer sheet. Two marks are given for each correct answer in **Parts 1 and 2** and one mark is given for each correct answer in **Part 3**. The total score is then weighted to 40 marks for the whole Reading paper.

Paper 2   Writing

General Impression Mark Scheme

A General Impression Mark Scheme is used in conjunction with a Task-specific Mark Scheme, which focuses on criteria specific to each particular task. The General Impression Mark Scheme summarises the content, organisation and cohesion, range of structures and vocabulary, register and format, and target reader indicated in each task.

A summary of the General Impression Mark Scheme is given below. Trained examiners, who are co-ordinated prior to each examination session, work with a more detailed version, which is subject to updating. The FCE General Impression Mark Scheme is interpreted at Council of Europe, Common European Framework Level B2.

Band 5	For a **Band 5** to be awarded, the candidate's writing fully achieves the desired effect on the target reader. All the content points required in the task are included* and expanded appropriately. Ideas are organised effectively, with the use of a variety of linking devices and a wide range of structure and vocabulary. The language is well developed, and any errors that do occur are minimal and perhaps due to ambitious attempts at more complex language. Register and format are consistently appropriate to the purpose of the task and the audience.
Band 4	For a **Band 4** to be awarded, the candidate's writing achieves the desired effect on the target reader. All the content points required in the task are included.* Ideas are clearly organised, with the use of suitable linking devices and a good range of structure and vocabulary. Generally, the language is accurate, and any errors that do occur are mainly attempts at more complex language. Register and format which are, on the whole, appropriate to the purpose of the task and the audience.
Band 3	For a **Band 3** to be awarded, the candidate's writing, on the whole achieves the desired effect on the target reader. All the content points required in the task are included.* Ideas are organised adequately, with the use of simple linking devices and an adequate range of structure and vocabulary. A number of errors may be present, but they do not impede communication. A reasonable, if not always successful, attempt is made at register and format which are appropriate to the purpose of the task and the audience.
Band 2	For a **Band 2** to be awarded, the candidate's writing does not clearly communicate the message to the target reader. Some content points required in the task are inadequately covered or omitted, and/or there is some irrelevant material. Ideas are inadequately organised, linking devices are rarely used, and the range of structure and vocabulary is limited. Errors distract the reader and may obscure communication at times. Attempts at appropriate register and format are unsuccessful or inconsistent.

Band 1	For a **Band 1** to be awarded, the candidate's writing has a very negative effect on the target reader. There is notable omission of content points and/or considerable irrelevance, possibly due to misinterpretation of the task. There is a lack of organisation or linking devices, and there is little evidence of language control. The range of structure and vocabulary is narrow and frequent errors obscure communication. There is little or no awareness of appropriate register and format.
Band 0	For a **Band zero** to be awarded, there is either too little language for assessment or the candidate's writing is totally irrelevant or totally illegible.

*Candidates who do not address all the content points will be penalised for dealing inadequately with the requirements of the task.

Candidates who fully satisfy the **Band 3** descriptor are likely to demonstrate an adequate performance in writing at FCE level.

Paper 2 sample answers and examiner's comments

The following pieces of writing have been selected from students' answers. The samples relate to tasks in Tests 1–4. Explanatory notes have been added to show how the bands have been arrived at. The comments should be read in conjunction with the task-specific mark schemes included in the Keys.

Sample A (Test 1, Question 2 – Essay)

> I am a egologist person and me and my family take care of the environment and so we use public transport. Nowadays, there is a lot of pollution and we have a lot of enviroment problem like greenhouse effect ozone hole. The car is one of the environment problems.
>
> Almost all people use care because is more convenient. Why? Because when we need move we don't have to wait the public transport, we don't have to change bus or train. But there are a lot of advantages to take public transport. First of all, it is four our future, less pollution!
>
> Sometimes the public transport are quickly than car, during the travel you can read, sleep, speak with other people. If we take a special card is not so expansive and is less dangerous for the accident.
>
> Disadvantages for the car: the fuel is expansive, a lot of traffic and a lot of danger in the street.
>
> My slogan is less car, less pollution, better life.
>
> Finally, I think in the future we will use more public transport than the car.

Comments

Content
Good range of appropriate vocabulary.

Organisation and cohesion
Ideas inadequately organised. Poor linking.

Range
Ambitious but unsuccessful.

Accuracy
Frequent errors, which distract the reader.

Appropriacy of register and format
Suitably neutral register but poor linking.

Target reader
Would understand the message but be distracted by the number of errors.

Band: 2

Sample B (Test 1, Question 4 – Review)

> *Last year I travelled in England with my familie, and we stayed in one very nice hotel. It was small and the owner was a man, Mr Brown, and his wife.*
>
> *My parents had a double room and my sister and I shared a room which it had two beds. We had a balconie which we could see the sea. Our rooms were very confortable and we had televisions which my sister and me watched sometimes in the evening wen there was a good film.*
>
> *The were two very good things about the hotel. first, the owner who was kind to us and very funny. Nothing was too difficult for him, and he was always helpful. Then there was the owner's wife who was such a good cooker! Every morning we had wonderful breakfast with eggs and bacon and sausages. So my parents decided we could eat there in the evenings also and she asked to us what we will like to eat. it was great!*
>
> *So if you go to Banbridge, you should go to this Star Hotel. I am sure you will enjoy it very very much.*

Comments

Content
Reasonable achievement of the task set.

Organisation and cohesion
Ideas adequately organised, with simple linking devices.

Range
Adequate.

Accuracy
Errors present, but they do not impede communication.

Appropriacy of register and format
Reasonably appropriate to purpose and audience.

Target reader
Would be informed.

Band: 3

Sample C (Test 2, Question 1 – Email)

Hi Peter,

Thanks very much for your email. It's been ages since we saw each other, hasn't it?

Anyway, of course I have lots of ideas for Anna's birthday party. Your idea about the Majestic Hotel sounds great, but what about the price? I'm not sure whether it's too expensive or not.

Well, don't worry about her present. Anna loves travelling, so I think it'd be a good idea to give her a trip, which she can choose.

Anyway, I've bad news for you because I'm very busy the day before the party, so I can't help you with the preparations. I'm very sorry! I hope you'll find someone else giving you a hand. Maybe Brian.

To make the party special, we could organise a Karaoke party. I remember how much fun she had at the last visit in the Karaoke Bar. That'll be a great surprise for Anna.

So, please let me know what you think.

Love,

Comments

Content
All points covered with good expansion.

Organisation and cohesion
Well organised and linked.

Range
Good range with natural tone.

Accuracy
Very accurate.

Appropriacy of register and format
Very appropriate and natural.

Target reader
A convincing email which informs the target reader.

Band: 5

Sample D (Test 2, Question 2 – Essay)

In the past, young people used to wear their parents clothes, so that they would look like they were older. The truth is, that nowadays, young people, always want to dress differently from their parents.

It seems that to them, that their parents' clothes are 'old-fashioned' and are worn only by the 'old people'. These suits of the young men's fathers, look as they say, like if they were going to a funeral and these dresses of the young women' mothers look like if they were made 'in the wild west'.

And if young people don't wear clothes like their parents', what kind of clothes do they wear and why? Nowadays, young people have a tendency to wear informal clothes, especially really large jeans and T-shirts. The clothes that young men wear don't differ a lot from the young women's. The only exception is, that young women tend to wear really tight trousers and blouses. In my opinion, they want to wear these clothes in order to make a revolution, as they are recieving a lot of pressure from their parents.

In conclusion, young people always want to dress differently from their parents and that's what they really do.

Comments

Content
Good realisation of the task.

Organisation and cohesion
Ideas clearly organised with some linking.

Range
Good range of vocabulary and structure.

Accuracy
Good – but some minor errors.

Appropriacy of register and format
Consistently appropriate.

Target reader
Would be informed.

Band: 4

Sample E (Test 3, Question 1 – Letter)

Dear Kate,

How are you? I hope everything will be all right. If I were you I would go to Castle and lake Trips. It's really nice for a day trip. I went there and it was fantastic.

The departures can be 8am or 10a.m. daily but I recommend you at 8am because there are less people and it's better.

The first stop is at Bourne Castle. There is a beatiful Castle and is important to get a tour because they will explain to everybody the Castle's history. After the lunch. You can choose take a picnic instead of a restaurant. It's cheaper. During the afternoon you will go to a beautiful lake where you can play water sports like water-motorcycles. It's really funny! The prices are good and also you can get reductions for groups, minimum 15 people.

I hope this information will be enough for you to consider this trip.

Best wishes

Comments

Content
All points covered.

Organisation and cohesion
Adequate; some reasonable linking.

Range
Adequate.

Accuracy
A number of non-impeding errors.

Appropriacy of register and format
Appropriate.

Target reader
Would be informed.

Band: 3

Sample F (Test 3, Question 4 – Article)

> <u>Could you live without television for a week?</u>
>
> That's a good question! It seems very easy just to turn off the TV set and spend your time better. But you have to realise that you must find something instead watching TV. I think before you start your first week without TV you must plan your activity. You will see how many things you can do during your new free time. You can for example do something for your health and fitness – you can go swimming, play tennis or go cycling. You can meet your friends, call parents or just do your room. You will be able to read more books or find new hobby. You will see that life is not just TV! I tried to live without television and now I enjoy my life much better. So don't think too long – try!

Comments

Content
Good realisation of the task.

Organisation and cohesion
Appropriate to article format.

Range
Good range within the task set; some repetition.

Accuracy
Minimal errors.

Appropriacy of register and format
Appropriate.

Target reader
Would be informed.

Band: 4

Sample G (Test 4, Question 4 – Story)

It was dangerous, but I knew I had to do it. It was a new challenge and not only for me but for everyone there.
Nobody thought I was capable of doing it.
I wasn't sure of what to do, and the pressure of everyone watching me was driving me mad.

Finally, I managed to move my right foot closer to the edge. I could listen to the crowd shouting 'to go'. That was my only chance. Only a few more seconds, otherwise my time would be over.

I didn't even think of looking down. I was already paralysed, and that would help me at all.

Then, by some 'strange power' my left foot was moving and I wanted to stop it, but it was too difficult.

The clock was running tic tac. And suddenly everything stopped. I felt an enormous peace. Somehow I managed to jump out of the airplane and I was flying!

Those minutes, up in the air, feeling the wind in my face, were fantastic. And then I was terrified when I couldn't open the parachute! Fortunately, I wasn't alone.

Comments

Content
Good storyline clearly linked to the prompt sentence.

Organisation and cohesion
Ideas effectively organised.

Range
A wide range of structure and vocabulary.

Accuracy
Minimal errors.

Appropriacy of register and format
Appropriate use of narrative technique for suspense.

Target reader
Would be able to follow the storyline.

Band: 5

Sample H (Test 4, Question 5b – Letter)

Dear kate,
I have'nt read the book of Pride and Predudice but I saw the film last week. I think it is beautiful story. I liked it very much.
  I think the reason why it is still a good story is numerous.
  Firstly, in the film, as in the book I think, Mr Darcy is so handsome that you can think of him like a famous star from the TV today! His love story is not easy – just like all the film and drama on TV today. You can imagine them true.
  Also the sisters in the story are very like in real life. But the mother is not very nice person. I think she is silly person and we can all know someone like her. All young people think that their parents do not know anything and so it is very much like real life.
  I recommend you to see the film of this story. I think it's the perfect way to spend some free time.
Lots of love
Daisy

Comments

Content
Good realisation of the task.

Organisation and cohesion
Clear organisation of ideas, with suitable paragraphing and linking.

Range
A range of structure shown and evidence of a good range of vocabulary.

Appropriacy of register and format
Consistent register suitable to the situation and target reader.

Target reader
Would be informed.

Band: 4

Paper 3   Use of English

One mark is given for each correct answer in **Parts 1, 2** and **3**. For **Part 4**, candidates are awarded a mark of 2, 1 or 0 for each question according to the accuracy of their response. Correct spelling is required in **Parts 2, 3** and **4**. The total mark is subsequently weighted to 40.

Paper 4   Listening

One mark is given for each correct answer. The total is weighted to give a mark out of 40 for the paper. In **Part 2** minor spelling errors are allowed, provided that the candidate's intention is clear.
  For security reasons, several versions of the Listening paper are used at each administration of the examination. Before grading, the performance of the candidates in each of the versions is compared and marks adjusted to compensate for any imbalance in levels of difficulty.

Paper 5   Speaking

Candidates are assessed on their own individual performance and not in relation to each other, according to the following four analytical critera: grammar and vocabulary, discourse management, pronunciation and interactive communication. Assessment is based on performance in the whole test and not in particular parts of the test.

Both examiners assess the candidates. The assessor applies detailed, analytical scales, and the interlocutor applies a global achievement scale, which is based on the analytical scales.

Analytical scores

Grammar and Vocabulary

This refers to the accurate and appropriate use of a range of grammatical forms and vocabulary. Performance is viewed in terms of the overall effectiveness of the language used in spoken interaction.

Discourse Management

This refers to the candidate's ability to link utterances together to form coherent speech, without undue hesitation. The utterances should be relevant to the tasks and should be arranged logically to develop the themes or arguments required by the tasks.

Pronunciation

This refers to the candidate's ability to produce intelligible utterances to fulfil the task requirements. This includes stress and intonation as well as individual sounds. Examiners put themselves in the position of the non-ESOL specialist and assess the overall impact of the pronunciation and the degree of effort required to understand the candidate.

Interactive Communication

This refers to the candidate's ability to take an active part in the development of the discourse. This requires the ability to participate in the range of interactive situations in the test and to develop discussions on a range of topics by initiating and responding appropriately. This also refers to the deployment of strategies to maintain interaction at an appropriate level throughout the test so that the tasks can be fulfilled.

Global Achievement

This refers to the candidate's overall effectiveness in dealing with the tasks in the four separate parts of the FCE Speaking test. The global mark is an independent, impression mark which reflects the assessment of the candidate's performance from the interlocutor's perspective.

Marks

Marks for each of the criteria are awarded out of a nine-point scale. Marks for the Speaking test are subsequently weighted to produce a final mark out of 40.

FCE typical minimum adequate performance

Although there are some inaccuracies, grammar and vocabulary are sufficiently accurate in dealing with the tasks. The language is mostly coherent, with some extended discourse. Candidates can generally be understood. They are able to maintain the interaction and deal with the tasks without major prompting.

Test 1 Key

Paper 1 **Reading** (1 hour)

Part 1

1 A   2 B   3 D   4 D   5 B   6 B   7 C   8 D

Part 2

9 E   10 H   11 F   12 A   13 C   14 G   15 D

Part 3

16 A   17 B   18 A   19/20 A/B (in either order)   21 E   22 B
23/24 D/E (in either order)   25/26 B/E (in either order)   27/28 A/E (in either order)
29/30 C/E (in either order)

Paper 2 **Writing** (1 hour 20 minutes)

Task-specific Mark Schemes

Part 1

Question 1

Content
The letter must include all the points in the notes:
1) say why learning English is important
2) say where group would prefer to stay and why
3) give information about the group's interests
4) ask about weather and/or clothing.

Organisation and cohesion
Clear organisation of ideas, with suitable paragraphing and linking, and opening/closing formulae as appropriate to the task.

Appropriacy of register and format
Consistent register appropriate to the situation and target reader.

Range
Language relating to the functions above. Vocabulary relating to the visit.

Target reader
Would be informed.

Part 2

Question 2

Content
Essay should agree or disagree with the statement, or discuss both sides of the argument.

Organisation and cohesion
Clear organisation of ideas, with suitable paragraphing and linking.

Appropriacy of register and format
Consistent register suitable to the situation and target reader.

Range
Language of describing, explaining and giving opinions.

Target reader
Would be informed.

Question 3

Content
Article should give information about one of the four ideas given for a club and say why the writer is choosing that idea. There should also be one other idea for a club with the reason for suggesting that idea.

Organisation and cohesion
Clear organisation of ideas, with suitable paragraphing and linking.

Appropriacy of register and format
Consistent register suitable to the situation and target reader.

Range
Language of describing, explaining and giving opinion.

Target reader
Would be informed.

Question 4

Content
Review should describe the hotel, and say why the writer did or did not enjoy staying there.

Organisation and cohesion
Clear organisation of ideas, with suitable paragraphing and linking.

Appropriacy of register and format
Consistent register suitable to the situation and target reader.

Range
Language of describing, explaining and giving opinion.

Test 1 Key

Target reader
Would be informed.

Question 5(a)

Content
Essay should answer the question and show understanding of the story.

Organisation and cohesion
Clear organisation of ideas, with suitable paragraphing and linking.

Appropriacy of register and format
Consistent register suitable to the situation and target reader.

Range
Language of describing, explaining and expressing opinion.
Vocabulary relating to crime.

Target reader
Would be informed.

Question 5(b)

Content
Letter should answer the question and show understanding of the story.

Organisation and cohesion
Clear organisation of ideas, with suitable paragraphing and linking.

Appropriacy of register and format
Consistent register suitable to the situation and target reader.

Range
Language of describing, explaining and expressing opinion.
Vocabulary relating to character.

Target reader
Would be informed.

Paper 3   Use of English (45 minutes)

Part 1

1 A   2 D   3 B   4 C   5 B   6 C   7 A   8 C   9 D
10 B   11 B   12 C

Part 2

13 which   14 so   15 the   16 would/might   17 something   18 for
19 with   20 without   21 up   22 to   23 had   24 as

Part 3

25 variety   26 director   27 inhabitants   28 choice/choices   29 growth
30 unemployment   31 agreement   32 loss   33 unable   34 decision

Part 4

35 **until** | we had finished/done   36 was **better** | than Tim   37 if | she **does** not do OR
unless | she **does**   38 if/whether he realised | **what** time   39 **put** an advertisement | for
40 **finished** his speech | before thanking   41 has been / is | a **month** since   42 **following**
their | appearance

Paper 4   Listening (approximately 40 minutes)

Part 1

1 A   2 A   3 C   4 B   5 C   6 B   7 C   8 A

Part 2

9 graves   10 twelfth century   11 their/the owners   12 make(-)up
13 ten thousand pounds   14 original clothes   15 soft bodies
16 maker(')s name(s)   17 (little) adults   18 plastic

Part 3

19 E   20 F   21 D   22 B   23 C

Part 4

24 B   25 C   26 B   27 B   28 C   29 A   30 C

Transcript   *This is the Cambridge First Certificate in English Listening Test. Test One.*

I'm going to give you the instructions for this test. I'll introduce each part of the test and give you time to look at the questions. At the start of each piece you'll hear this sound:

tone

You'll hear each piece twice.

Remember, while you're listening, write your answers on the question paper. You'll have five minutes at the end of the test to copy your answers onto the separate answer sheet.

There will now be a pause. Please ask any questions now, because you must not speak during the test.

[pause]

Now open your question paper and look at Part One.

[pause]

PART 1 *You'll hear people talking in eight different situations. For questions 1 to 8, choose the best answer, A, B or C.*

Question 1 *One.*
You hear part of a radio play.
Where is the scene taking place?
A in the street
B in a bank
C in a police station

[pause]

tone

Policeman:	So what happened, madam?
Woman:	Well, I saw this old man, he was kind of holding this briefcase under his arm, like this. He'd just left the bank and I was still queuing up to collect my pension, but I was near that door. Now, this young man came running past him and grabbed him by the arm.
Policeman:	And they both fell down?
Woman:	Yeah, and the young man ran away and the poor old man sat on the pavement, still clutching his briefcase, and we managed to help him up. Now, can I go back in to collect my money?
Policeman:	Would you mind coming with us, madam? We need a few more details.

[pause]

tone

[The recording is repeated.]

[pause]

Question 2 *Two.*
You overhear the beginning of a lecture.
What subject are the students taking?
A medicine
B sport
C music

[pause]

tone

It's important that you really listen to what people are telling you. For example, I had a trumpet player who came to see me with back pain and breathing difficulties. He couldn't take his final exams because of the muscular tension in his jaw, but when I quizzed him about it, it turned out that the actual problem was in his teeth – far away from where the pain actually was. The same applies to sports people who often have injuries as a result of their job …

[pause]

tone

[The recording is repeated.]

[pause]

Question 3

Three.
You overhear a conversation in a college.
Who is the young man?
A a new student
B a student in the middle of a course
C a former student

[pause]

tone

Man: It all looks so different. Where's the canteen?
Woman: It's in the basement. You get there by going down the main staircase from the entrance hall.
Man: Right. I'll get there in the end. Everything seems to have moved around.
Woman: Yes, there was a rebuilding programme last year, which wasn't much fun for those of us trying to study. The main building was altered a lot. And they're building a new sports centre. It should be open for the new students in September.
Man: Well, I'm envious. Everything looks a lot better.

[pause]

tone

[The recording is repeated.]

[pause]

Question 4

Four.
You hear a woman on the radio talking about a cookbook.
What does she regret?
A not looking after it
B not having kept it
C not using it properly

[pause]

tone

I used to watch Granny cooking, and right from when I was five years old I was allowed to season the soups, test the potatoes, and so on. One year for my birthday, she bought me a cookbook. It was just like Granny talking; all the recipes were simple, economical and linked with little stories, useful advice and amusing sketches. I treasured it, but gradually it fell to bits from overuse, my tastes changed and, finally, I threw it out. Now, of course, I wish I'd hung on to it despite its sad state and despite the fact that all the advice would be out of date.

[pause]

tone

[The recording is repeated.]

[pause]

Question 5

Five.
You hear someone talking about the day he met someone famous.
How did he feel after meeting Chris Turner?
A unimpressed with the footballer
B angry with his friend
C disappointed with himself

[pause]

tone

I went to a party with a friend and she knows that I'm a big fan of Chris Turner, the footballer. I just think he's a genius and, anyway, he was going to be there. Now, I knew that I would be really shy, which is stupid because he's exactly the same age as me and, you know, he's just a regular bloke, I'm sure. But when my friend introduced us and he shook my hand, my mouth just went, you know, really dry and I didn't know what to say, honestly, which was awful. I felt so bad about it afterwards, my friend just couldn't understand it.

[pause]

tone

[The recording is repeated.]

[pause]

Question 6

Six.
You hear a woman talking on the phone.
Why has she called?
A to request a meeting
B to offer assistance
C to apologise for her absence

[pause]

tone

Hi, can I just talk to you about our plans for the summer conference? I think I said that I was going to be away for the opening meeting and couldn't give you a hand, but it seems I got my diary muddled up and I will actually be around, so what would you like me to do?

[pause]

tone

[The recording is repeated.]

[pause]

Question 7   *Seven.*
You overhear an extract from a radio play.
What is the young woman's relationship with the man?
A She's a pupil of his.
B She's a relative of his.
C She's a patient of his.

[pause]

tone

Man: So, Sophie, tell me all about it.
Woman: I'm sorry, but I've just been feeling terrible for the last week or so and last night I just couldn't do my homework, I felt so bad. I was aching all over. So my dad said I had better make an appointment and come and see you. Perhaps you can tell me what's wrong.

[pause]

tone

[The recording is repeated.]

[pause]

Question 8   *Eight.*
You hear someone telling a story about a strange thing that happened in the mountains.
What point does the story prove?
A how strange things can be explained simply
B how easy it is to imagine things
C how you can be tricked by the silence

[pause]

tone

My wife Margaret and I were sitting behind a rock on the top of a mountain in the Highlands one day, nobody else around, perfectly silent, and Margaret said, 'I just heard a telephone bell ringing.' 'Oh,' I said, 'Margaret, there are no telephone kiosks up here.' But in the silence of the hills, you can imagine anything. I said, 'I often imagine things. I've heard babies crying in this silence. I've thought I heard a symphony orchestra,' and Margaret said, 'I'm sure I heard a telephone ringing.' She got up and went round the back of the rock and there was a cow with a bell around its neck.

[pause]

tone

[The recording is repeated.]

[pause]

That's the end of Part One.

Now turn to Part Two.

[pause]

PART 2 *You'll hear part of a talk about dolls. For questions 9 to 18, complete the sentences.*

You now have forty-five seconds in which to look at Part Two.

[pause]

tone

Dolls have always fascinated me, and that's why, five years ago, I was delighted to be offered the job of running a doll museum.

Dolls have existed for thousands of years, and the earliest dolls we know about were found in graves in ancient Egypt. I only wish we could get one or two for our museum, but we haven't unfortunately got anything as old as that in the museum. All the same, we have got examples from Europe from the twelfth century, but my favourite early dolls are actually from the seventeenth century. They interest me not just because they are early, or fairly early, but also because of the clothes they're wearing. They have their original clothes, and from them we know what the owners wore, since dolls in those days were always dressed like their owners. They were made of the only material readily available for things like this at the time: solid wood, and they were painted in great detail. In fact, on the best examples, like the ones in the museum, the detail includes the seventeenth-century make-up.

Dolls like these were very expensive then, and only the very rich could afford them. These days, they're popular with collectors and if you want one today, you have to pay anything up to ten thousand pounds for a doll in perfect condition from this time! By the way, what makes them so valuable is that, as far as a collector is concerned, a doll is only worth collecting if it is in perfect condition, and that means having the original clothes.

Doll collecting has become very fashionable since the museum opened, with people interested in dolls from every period, including later dolls. There's great interest in nineteenth-century examples, when dolls were no longer made of wood, but began to have soft bodies and real hair. They were very delicate and few have survived, meaning such a doll would be worth about two thousand pounds, perhaps a bit more. Later, in the nineteenth century, you could often take off the doll's hair. If you can, you can often see the maker's name underneath, and of course the right one increases a doll's value.

There was a really big change in dolls at the beginning of the twentieth century. In the museum we have one of the earliest examples, from about 1909, of a doll that's a model of a baby. Previously all dolls, the earlier ones, were little adults. That's just one of the changes that have occurred in the last hundred years. Another, again, is to do with what dolls are made of. Although dolls with soft bodies continued, after about 1930, plastic began to be used. In fact, dolls from the 1930s and 40s are now very popular with collectors, some of them selling for very, very high prices.

[pause]

Now you'll hear Part Two again.

tone

[The recording is repeated.]

[pause]

That's the end of Part Two.

Now turn to Part Three.

[pause]

PART 3   *You'll hear five different people talking about why they decided to become nurses. For questions 19 to 23, choose which of the reasons, A to F, each speaker is giving. Use the letters only once. There is one extra letter which you do not need to use.*

You now have thirty seconds in which to look at Part Three.

[pause]

tone

Speaker One

[pause]

Well I have to say, I never really thought about a career until I got to my last year at school. Lots of people here say that they knew exactly what they wanted to do right from a very young age, but I never really had any burning ambitions. In the end I just sort of drifted into it because that's what our lot have always done. If I'd chosen something else – like going into business, say – I would have been the first for four generations to have gone outside the medical field. I don't think that that would have mattered but it means there are lots of things we can talk about at home.

[pause]

Speaker Two

[pause]

Most of my friends went into teaching actually – I think they felt it was more 'academic' and of course the pay is quite a bit better. But I've never really been bothered about things like that – I think the enjoyment of the job comes first and I certainly get a lot of good feelings doing this work. We have some difficult cases sometimes but there's still a lot of laughter here and the patients can be amazing – especially the kids. I'd recommend it to anyone who likes helping people.

[pause]

Speaker Three

[pause]

I think I'm lucky really because I didn't try very hard at school – I guess you'd call me lazy! And then it ended and I thought, 'Wow, I'd better think about a job,' and I got really worried and emotional about it because, well, I suddenly realised that I didn't want to go from job to job, you know. I wanted a career and regular money and an opportunity to climb up the ladder if possible. So, one day I saw a TV programme about nursing and it looked like it had the kind of benefits that I wanted – so here I am.

[pause]

Speaker Four

[pause]

At first I thought I'd made the wrong choice … you know, I was never really sure that it was the thing for me and I used to go back to my flat at night and think, 'Well maybe I should have listened to my parents after all'. They thought I'd get too upset and that I should have stuck with something office-based like the rest of my family but it was my best subject at school – well Biology was – and all the staff there thought medicine would be a good choice, so …
Anyway, one day I woke up and felt fine about it and it's been great ever since.

[pause]

Speaker Five

[pause]

I remember we all had to go to this Careers Advisor in our last year at school and I think she got really confused when she saw me because I just had no idea. I liked the sound of a lot of jobs and I couldn't make up my mind. When the time came to tell our teachers what we were going to apply for, I thought, 'Well what *does* matter to me is being separate from my friends' and so I went round to see one of them – the most important I suppose, and anyway she had chosen nursing, so that was it really – a difficult decision made easy, although I must say, I've never regretted it.

[pause]

Now you'll hear Part Three again.

tone

[The recording is repeated.]

[pause]

That's the end of Part Three.

Now turn to Part Four.

[pause]

PART 4   *You'll hear an interview with someone who works in the film industry. For questions 24 to 30, choose the best answer, A, B or C.*

You now have one minute in which to look at Part Four.

[pause]

tone

Interviewer: I suppose the first question I have to ask you, Alan, is one you get fed up answering, but here goes: what is a Best Boy?

Alan: Well, I'm not sure why I'm called a Best Boy exactly, but I like to think it's because I'm the best at what I do. But the title is an American term used to describe the assistant to the man who works with the cameramen and the electricians on a film to make sure that the film is properly lit.

Interviewer: So how do you spend your time?

Alan: Basically what I do is work between the electrical department and production. I deal with the companies where the lights come from. And I'm also there on the film set, making sure that everything runs smoothly, that the lighting is set up when the camera crew arrives to shoot the film, and then I also help with the budget – we have to do timesheets, things like that. It's mostly paperwork really.

Interviewer: When did you start working in the industry?

Alan: About fifteen years ago. I'd been an electrician and my first few film jobs were basic electrical ones, then I moved over to this.

Interviewer: It sounds a rather complicated job to me.

Alan: No, not really. I've never had to do anything out of the ordinary. But filming on location does make things more intense – there's less control than in the studio and you can have problems with the weather. On my latest film, we were working in the hills and it would take us ages to get the equipment up there. But I enjoyed it. It was a challenge.

Interviewer: Is working on location a plus for you?

Alan: Well, you see some great places, but long working days and problems with production are far more common. There's a lot of responsibility with the job, because there's so much money involved. If all the lighting goes wrong on one day, then obviously there'll be trouble. The long hours are very unsociable, which is OK if you're single, but there's quite a lot of work abroad, which puts a lot of pressure on the family. I went away for five months once. When I left, my son wasn't talking, and when I came back, he was. It varies though. Some years you don't go away at all.

Interviewer: What advice would you give to someone wanting to give it a try?

Alan: You need a good head for mathematics, plus knowing how to mend a fuse. So training as an electrician is the first step, then you need some experience on the production floor.

Interviewer: Where do you see yourself in the future? What would promotion be for you?

Alan: I like it where I am. I like working behind the scenes and seeing how the production works. There are enough challenges in the present job for me. The more experience you get, the more you worry whether you've got things to the right stage at the right time or not. You can't just go home and switch off. But getting things right is a big satisfaction.

[pause]

Now you'll hear Part Four again.

tone

[The recording is repeated.]

[pause]

That's the end of Part Four.

There'll now be a pause of five minutes for you to copy your answers onto the separate answer sheet. Be sure to follow the numbering of all the questions. I'll remind you when there is one minute left, so that you're sure to finish in time.

[Teacher, pause the recording here for five minutes. Remind your students when they have one minute left.]

That's the end of the test. Please stop now. Your supervisor will now collect all the question papers and answer sheets.

Test 2 Key

Paper 1   Reading (1 hour)

Part 1

1 B   2 B   3 D   4 C   5 A   6 A   7 D   8 C

Part 2

9 H   10 F   11 A   12 C   13 G   14 D   15 E

Part 3

16 E   17 D   18 A   19 D   20/21 C/E (in either order)   22 B   23 E
24/25. A/B (in either order)   26 C   27/28 B/D (in either order)   29 C   30 D

Paper 2   Writing (1 hour 20 minutes)

Task-specific Mark Schemes

Part 1

Question 1

Content
The email must include all the points in the notes:
1) comment on the hotel / having the party in the hotel
2) suggest a present for Anna
3) apologise for not being able to help the day before the party
4) suggest something else for the party.

Organisation and cohesion
Clear organisation of ideas, with suitable paragraphing and linking, and opening/closing formulae as appropriate to the task.

Appropriacy of register and format
Standard English appropriate to the situation and target reader, observing grammar and spelling conventions.

Range
Language relating to the functions above.
Vocabulary relating to parties and arrangements.

Target reader
Would be informed.

Part 2

Question 2

Content
Essay should agree or disagree with the statement, or discuss both sides of the argument.

Organisation and cohesion
Clear organisation of ideas, with suitable paragraphing and linking.

Appropriacy of register and format
Consistent register suitable to the situation and target reader.

Range
Language of describing, explaining and giving opinion.
Vocabulary relating to clothes and fashion.

Target reader
Would be informed.

Question 3

Content
Letter should explain why the writer is a suitable person for the job.

Organisation and cohesion
Clear organisation of ideas, with suitable paragraphing and linking.

Appropriacy of register and format
Consistent register suitable to the situation and target reader.

Range
Language of explanation, giving information and personal description.

Target reader
Would be informed.

Question 4

Content
Story should follow from the prompt sentence.

Organisation and cohesion
Clear organisation of ideas, with suitable paragraphing and linking.

Appropriacy of register and format
Consistent register suitable to the situation and target reader.

Range
Narrative tenses. Vocabulary relating to the chosen topic of the story.

Target reader
Would be informed.

Question 5(a)

Content
Article should give the writer's opinion about the importance of truth and lies in the story.

Organisation and cohesion
Clear organisation of ideas, with suitable paragraphing and linking.

Appropriacy of register and format
Consistent register suitable to the situation and target reader.

Range
Language of describing, explaining and giving opinion.
Vocabulary relating to topic and storyline.

Target reader
Would be informed.

Question 5(b)

Content
Essay should explain how Lizzy's feelings for Darcy change.

Organisation and cohesion
Clear organisation of ideas, with suitable paragraphing and linking.

Appropriacy of register and format
Consistent register suitable to the situation and target reader.

Range
Language of describing, explaining and giving opinion.
Vocabulary relating to character and relationships.

Target reader
Would be informed.

Paper 3 Use of English (45 minutes)

Part 1

1 C   2 B   3 C   4 B   5 D   6 B   7 A   8 B   9 A   10 A
11 D   12 C

Part 2

13 because   14 more   15 of   16 too   17 be/sound   18 when/while/as
19 which   20 what   21 again   22 if/provided   23 first   24 by

Part 3

25 frequently   26 impressive   27 comfortable   28 flight
29 connections   30 increasingly   31 improvement(s)
32 noisy   33 crowded/overcrowded   34 unfortunately

Part 4

35 would **like** | to know   36 **let** us | park (our car)   37 if | I had **seen**
38 **there** is | a hole in   39 pays (any/much) **attention** | to
40 if she | would **lend** him OR to | **lend** him   41 **might** have | forgotten
42 (single) child | has (great) **fun**

Paper 4 Listening (approximately 40 minutes)

Part 1

1 A   2 A   3 C   4 B   5 A   6 B   7 C   8 C

Part 2

9 camping   10 fit (your back)   11 (a) day(-)trip / one-day trips / one day / day(-)trips
12 climb (up)   13 solid/firm bottom / leather base   14 (two) compartment(s)
15 sharp   16 easy to adjust / easily adjusted / (easily) adjustable   17 falling (off)
18 (air)(-)hole(s) / airholes / ventilation

Part 3

19 F   20 B   21 A   22 E   23 C

Part 4

24 B   25 C   26 A   27 A   28 C   29 B   30 C

Transcript   *This is the Cambridge First Certificate in English Listening Test. Test Two.*

I'm going to give you the instructions for this test. I'll introduce each part of the test and give you time to look at the questions. At the start of each piece you'll hear this sound:

tone

You'll hear each piece twice.

Remember, while you're listening, write your answers on the question paper. You'll have five minutes at the end of the test to copy your answers onto the separate answer sheet.

There will now be a pause. Please ask any questions now, because you must not speak during the test.

[pause]

Now open your question paper and look at Part One.

[pause]

PART 1   *You'll hear people talking in eight different situations. For questions 1 to 8, choose the best answer, A, B or C.*

Question 1   *One.*
You overhear two people talking in a restaurant.
Where has the woman just come from?
A a supermarket
B a hospital
C a football match

[pause]

tone

Woman:	I felt so sorry for her, she just couldn't cope. She had the baby under one arm and a list in the other. And he was screaming, all red in the face. She must have only just come out of hospital, he was so tiny.
Man:	So you offered to help.
Woman:	Well, I wanted to get through the check-out and pay for my things quickly, otherwise I knew I'd be late getting here, but …
Man:	Well, I've only been here half an hour.
Woman:	Oh, I'm sorry, there was such a queue. And then I forgot, it's the big football game today and the roads were just packed …

[pause]

tone

[The recording is repeated.]

[pause]

Question 2   *Two.*
You hear a man talking about a mobile phone he has bought.
What most attracted him to this phone?
A its size
B its reliability
C its price

[pause]

tone

I've never wanted to walk around with an enormous mobile, you know, fixed to my belt or whatever, because that's socially embarrassing, isn't it? So I was really taken with the Edmundsen GP 876 model which you can just slip in your inside pocket and no one's the wiser, if you know what I mean. And it says in the blurb 'satisfaction guaranteed – should your mobile develop a fault in the first year, we will replace it the next day'. Well, to be honest, it wasn't exactly what you call cheap, so I'm rather hoping that I don't need to find out just how good that particular promise is.

[pause]

tone

[The recording is repeated.]

[pause]

Question 3

Three.
You hear a man talking on the phone about buying a house.
What is the purpose of his call?
A to apologise
B to complain
C to obtain information

[pause]

tone

Hello, it's Mr Brown here. I got your message. Yes, I was really sorry to hear the house I wanted had just been sold ... Yes ... I missed the chance to buy the house of my dreams. Yes, I know it wasn't your fault. I should have contacted you earlier ... Yes ... That's why I'm now eager to hear of any houses that come on the market. As you know, what I want is a house which combines a kitchen and breakfast room with lots of space for living, eating and cooking ... Yes, I'm tired of small places where you can hardly move.

[pause]

tone

[The recording is repeated.]

[pause]

Question 4

Four.
You hear a teenage girl talking about her hobby.
What is she talking about?
A a computer game
B a musical instrument
C a piece of sports equipment

[pause]

tone

I got it as a present from my father when I was fourteen. My family thought it would be a phase, that I'd go off the idea. Mum doesn't believe there'll be any money in it, but Dad is quite interested because, apart from football, it's the only thing I can talk to him about at the moment. If you're not going to make the effort to practise on it, no way is anyone going to be interested in you. I think one of the reasons you see so few girls playing in bands is that they tend not to be willing to do all that work.

[pause]

tone

[The recording is repeated.]

[pause]

Question 5

Five.
On the news, you hear a story about a cat.
Where was the cat found?
A in a train carriage
B on the railway lines
C on a station platform

[pause]

tone

A cat with a mind of its own joined the eleven fifty-five train from King's Lynn yesterday. A passenger spotted the cat, thought to have boarded at Littleport, and handed it to a member of the platform staff once the train got to Ely station. The friendly cat was put in a box and returned to Littleport. Eventually, its owner, Jack Prince, from Littleport, was reunited with his cat. It is thought that the cat must have crossed the lines at Littleport and waited on the platform, together with a dozen passengers who didn't notice it at all.

[pause]

tone

[The recording is repeated.]

[pause]

Question 6

Six.
You hear a woman talking about how she gets ideas for her work.
Who is the woman?
A a novelist
B an artist
C a film-maker

[pause]

tone

I work with my husband, Bob, and every time we have a holiday somewhere, we seem to come up with an idea. And touring round the USA last year, he'd written the words for this children's ghost story. But I had no idea how to … to get the atmosphere in the pictures, which is my role in the partnership. And then we went to Las Vegas and all that amazing architecture, lit up at night under the desert sky, was er … was dreamlike. I mean, despite all the films, nothing prepares you for what it actually feels like to be there. I just sat down and started sketching out ideas on the spot.

[pause]

tone

[The recording is repeated.]

[pause]

Question 7 | *Seven.*
You hear two people talking.
How does the woman feel?
A surprised
B satisfied
C relieved

[pause]

tone

Woman: | There they are! At last. I've been looking for them everywhere.
Man: | What? Your keys? You're always losing them.
Woman: | I know, and I really thought I'd lost them for good this time. Thank goodness!
Man: | Why don't you make sure you put them down in the same place, then you'd have the satisfaction of finding them whenever you wanted them.
Woman: | Maybe. That's not a bad idea. I'll think about it.

[pause]

tone

[The recording is repeated.]

[pause]

Question 8 | *Eight.*
You turn on the radio and hear a man speaking.
What are you listening to?
A a history programme
B a science-fiction story
C an advertisement

[pause]

tone

Discover the amazing secrets of the planet Earth in three major recently launched exhibitions: 'From the Beginning', 'Earth's Treasury' and 'Earth Today and Tomorrow', which form the finest series of exhibitions of their kind in the world. Together they tell Earth's dramatic story, starting with the birth of the universe, exploring the forces that shape it and the riches within it, concluding with a glimpse into the future and what it might hold for our planet.

[pause]

tone

[The recording is repeated.]

[pause]

That's the end of Part One.

Now turn to Part Two.

[pause]

PART 2   *You'll hear part of a radio programme about bags for walkers. For questions 9 to 18 complete the sentences.*

You now have forty-five seconds in which to look at Part Two.

[pause]

tone

Announcer: And now for a few tips for those of you who are going to go walking this summer. Let's look first of all at the type of bag that you should take with you. Rod Smith works in a shop that sells camping equipment and he feels he has a bag for every type of walking holiday. Rod, does it really make a difference what type of bag you use?

Rod: Yes, Jill, it certainly does. Bags come in every shape, colour and size now so it makes sense to pick one that is right for your needs. A backpack, for example, could quite rapidly ruin an otherwise good walking holiday if it doesn't fit your back. In fact the fit is critical but the choice is so large now that it's difficult to know *how* to make the right one. So – here are a few things to look for.

   First of all size. A bag that holds thirty-five litres and has three outside pockets should be plenty big enough for a day-trip. For a four to five-day walking tour I would recommend a bag that holds seventy litres for a man and fifty to sixty litres for a woman. That's along with a tent and a sleeping bag. An upright bag – that's one that closes at the top – is better if you intend to climb a lot of hills.

   What about the contents? Well, in order to really avoid the inconvenience of broken containers or crushed clothes, I suggest you go for a bag with a solid bottom. The best ones – but these are probably the most expensive – have a leather base that is particularly resistant to wear and tear. A bag that has two compartments inside will allow you to find things more easily and separate out items such as creams that could leak in hot weather. Extra pockets on the outside of the bag are also useful if you want to carry any tools for climbing that are sharp or get dirty when you use them.

   Then you have to think about carrying your bag. If it's a backpack, a wide, cushioned belt will ease the strain on your back and hips and leave you with more energy for your walking activities. Shoulder straps also help lighten the load and these should be easy to adjust. There are many different types of strap on the market that can be adjusted in various different ways. Try several and compare them. It's also a good idea to make sure there's a horizontal bar that goes across your shoulders and stops the straps from falling off.

Well, if you choose your bag carefully and think about some of the things I've mentioned, you shouldn't waste your money. Finally, make sure there are plenty of air holes in the padded part of your bag that touches your body. These are essential to allow sweat to escape and to make your walking or climbing holiday a comfortable one.

[pause]

Now you'll hear Part Two again.

tone

[The recording is repeated.]

[pause]

That's the end of Part Two.

Now turn to Part Three.

[pause]

PART 3

You will hear five different students who are studying away from home. They are talking about their accommodation. For questions 19 to 23, choose from the list, A to F, what each speaker says about their accommodation. Use the letters only once. There is one extra letter which you do not need to use.

You now have thirty seconds in which to look at Part Three.

[pause]

tone

Speaker One

[pause]

I'd requested college accommodation, so when I was offered it I was really pleased. I didn't fancy having to look after myself ... too many other things to do ... lessons and homework and going out with friends. I knew what the rules were – in by ten, no noise after nine – and I didn't mind them at first, but they've started to annoy me more and more – and now I can't wait to get out and be able to do my own thing. I don't think I'll be recommending this place to anyone else!

[pause]

Speaker Two

[pause]

It's exciting leaving home and becoming independent. I've been staying with some relatives for the past year. I'd stayed with them before so when I knew I was coming here to study they said, why don't you come and live with us –

great. And they've been fine – let me do whatever I want and haven't stuck to rigid meal times and all that sort of thing. So I've been able to meet plenty of people and get to know the area and the course and so on. I feel a part of it all now, but I'm always ready to try something different.

[pause]

Speaker Three

[pause]

I was pretty calm about coming here, but I couldn't decide whether to stay with a family or get my own flat. I'd talked to other people, you know, friends who've studied away from home before and they all recommended that I should get a flat because you have so much more freedom, so I did that. I'd only been here two weeks and I went out one day and left the front door unlocked. When I got back, I found that my camera had been stolen. I suppose I was lucky it was just that. I'm a bit more careful now.

[pause]

Speaker Four

[pause]

My friend Benny and I started the course at the same time. There was never any doubt that we'd share a place. It was the obvious choice for us to make and I think it's definitely the best option. Of course, you have to think about what you're going to eat, have some kind of system for cleaning, a few ground rules. We get annoyed with each other at times. Benny smokes and I had to ask him to go outside, which he does now. It hasn't all been straightforward but overall I prefer the independence this place gives me.

[pause]

Speaker Five

[pause]

My sister came here before me and studied at the same college. She told my parents that it would be much better if I stayed with her and then she could look after me, help me settle down here, that kind of thing. So, that's what happened – nobody asked me what I wanted to do. Well, the truth is we don't get on badly but I never seem to see the other students that I study with, which is a big disadvantage. I think it's better to force yourself to find your own way in a new environment.

[pause]

Now you'll hear Part Three again.

tone

[The recording is repeated.]

[pause]

That's the end of Part Three.

Now turn to Part Four.

[pause]

PART 4   *You will hear part of a radio interview in which Tina White, a magazine editor, talks about her life and work. For questions 24 to 30, choose the best answer A, B or C.*

You now have one minute in which to look at Part Four.

[pause]

tone

Interviewer: Tina White, some people describe you as the best magazine editor in the world, and you are only in your thirties. Can you tell us how you started your amazing career?

Tina: Well, when I was twenty, still at college, I was asked to write a weekly column for a local paper. The paper had wanted me to write about famous people, you know, their wonderful lifestyles, the sort of thing people like to read about. Instead, what I did was to concentrate on people who the general public didn't know, but who had something original to say.

Interviewer: And you got away with it! Now at that early stage, your family was important. How far did they influence your career choice?

Tina: My father was a film producer, and my childhood was spent around international actors and directors, so with such influences, I should have become an actress – something my father would have loved. But no, I chose to be a journalist in spite of the wishes of my family. I think the biggest influence was my school, not so much the people but the materials it gave me access to … the hours and hours spent in the library.

Interviewer: From being a journalist, you then went on to become an editor. I understand the first magazine you edited, *Female Focus*, wasn't much of a success?

Tina: Well, I was the editor for a year, and then I resigned, mainly because of disagreements with the owners. They were reluctant to change things, because they had faith it would eventually make a profit. But when you think of it, the magazine had been losing millions of pounds a year before I became its editor. When I left, it was still losing money but nothing like as much as previously. Also, when I took over, it was selling around six hundred and fifty thousand copies. That soon increased to eight hundred thousand, so it was certainly an improvement.

Interviewer: And now you are editing *Woman's World*, and you've made it the best-selling women's magazine ever. How do you make people want to read it?

Tina: For some of my competitors, the most important point is what you put on the cover of your magazine. But they forget faithful readers look beyond that. The real challenge is, how do you encourage a reader to read a serious piece? How are we going to make it an article that people want to read? You have to get their attention. And nothing does that better than a very lively, even shocking, opening line.

Interviewer: It is said that you work very hard because you don't trust your employees.

Tina: That *was* the case five years ago, when I was appointed. It almost drove me mad. I knew I had the right idea, for example, but I wasn't able to get it done because I didn't have the brilliant writers I have now, or the right staff to read all the material when it came in. I had to read everything about six times, and that was awful! It took me four years to put together the team I wanted, and it would be very unfair to say I don't trust them.

Interviewer: Do you sometimes worry that you might lose your fame and wealth?

Tina: Yes, when you work as an editor, you are praised today and criticised tomorrow. Of course it would be difficult to live without all the … well … material comforts I'm used to, but a smaller income is something I think I could cope with. It wouldn't be the end of the world. Much more serious would be if the people I work with no longer admired my work, and most of all I want it to stay that way.

Interviewer: And what about the future?

Tina: Well, people often think I have planned my career very carefully, but in fact lots of things have happened by chance. Lots of opportunities have come my way, and I was once asked to edit a book series. As a youngster, one of my dreams was to be a writer, to write a novel that would become a best-seller and then an award-winning film. Well, it may seem silly, but I still hope that will happen one day.

Interviewer: Tina, thank you very much for joining us today.

[pause]

Now you'll hear Part Four again.

tone

[The recording is repeated.]

[pause]

That's the end of Part Four.

There'll now be a pause of five minutes for you to copy your answers onto the separate answer sheet. Be sure to follow the numbering of all the questions. I'll remind you when there is one minute left, so that you're sure to finish in time.

[Teacher, pause the recording here for five minutes. Remind your students when they have one minute left.]

That's the end of the test. Please stop now. Your supervisor will now collect all the question papers and answer sheets.

Test 3 Key

Paper 1　Reading (1 hour)

Part 1

1 C　　2 A　　3 A　　4 B　　5 D　　6 C　　7 A　　8 B

Part 2

9 F　　10 H　　11 E　　12 A　　13 C　　14 G　　15 B

Part 3

16 A　　17 C　　18 D　　19 F　　20 B　　21/22 C/D (in either order)　　23 C
24 B　　25 E　　26 A　　27 E　　28/29 D/F (in either order)　　30 A

Paper 2　Writing (1 hour 20 minutes)

Task-specific Mark Schemes

Part 1

Question 1

Content
The letter must include all the points in the notes:
1) recommend the earlier trip, as it is less crowded
2) suggest taking a picnic and explain why
3) suggest trying water sport(s)
4) give information about numbers for group booking.

Organisation and cohesion
Clear organisation of ideas, with suitable paragraphing and linking, and opening/closing formulae as appropriate to the task.

Appropriacy of register and format
Consistent register appropriate to the situation and target reader.

Range
Language relating to the functions above.
Vocabulary relating to arrangements for boat trip.

Target reader
Would be informed.

Part 2

Question 2

Content
Report should give suggestions about how often the club should meet, what type of activities it should organise and how the club could be advertised.

Organisation and cohesion
Clear organisation of ideas, with suitable paragraphing and linking. Headings an advantage but not essential.

Appropriacy of register and format
Consistent register suitable to the situation and target reader.

Range
Language of suggestions and explanation.
Vocabulary relating to club and its activities.

Target reader
Would be informed.

Question 3

Content
Story should continue from prompt sentence.

Organisation and cohesion
Storyline should be clear. Paragraphing could be minimal.

Appropriacy of register and format
Consistent register suitable to the story.

Range
Narrative tenses. Vocabulary appropriate to the chosen topic of story.

Target reader
Would be able to follow the storyline.

Question 4

Content
Article should describe the difference it would make in the writer's life to have to live without television for a week.

Organisation and cohesion
Clear organisation of ideas, with suitable paragraphing and linking.

Appropriacy of register and format
Consistent register suitable to the situation and target reader.

Range
Language of description, explanation and comparison.
Vocabulary relating to television.

Target reader
Would be informed.

Question 5(a)

Content
Essay should explain the ways in which Mark helps Julie.

Organisation and cohesion
Clear organisation of ideas, with suitable paragraphing and linking.

Appropriacy of register and format
Consistent register suitable to the situation and target reader.

Range
Language of description and explanation.
Vocabulary relating to story and plot.

Target reader
Would be informed.

Question 5(b)

Content
Article should describe two unpleasant characters.

Organisation and cohesion
Clear organisation of ideas, with suitable paragraphing and linking.

Appropriacy of register and format
Consistent register suitable to the situation and target reader.

Range
Language of description and information.
Vocabulary relating to the storyline and characters.

Target reader
Would be informed.

Paper 3   Use of English (45 minutes)

Part 1

1 D   2 A   3 A   4 D   5 A   6 B   7 B   8 C   9 D   10 A
11 D   12 B

Part 2

13 did/tried   14 with/over   15 such   16 to   17 those
18 only/just   19 could/would   20 it   21 nothing   22 but/although
23 which   24 for

Part 3

25 attractive   26 tourists   27 achievement   28 employee
29 unclear   30 traditional   31 success   32 appearance
33 originality   34 communication(s)

Part 4

35 **my** holiday | I had   36 **ought** to | have locked   37 any **chance** | of Pete
38 from Paul | **nobody** has   39 got | **used** to   40 **felt** like | doing   41 being
unable | to sing   42 as **soon** as | we arrive

Paper 4   Listening (approximately 40 minutes)

Part 1

1 C   2 B   3 A   4 B   5 B   6 A   7 C   8 B

Part 2

9 south of France   10 1970   11 famous people   12 (young) children
13 (about) 50%   14 under (the) water   15 breathe (out)   16 (try to) float
17 (feeling) confident   18 3 hours/lessons

Part 3

19 C   20 B   21 D   22 F   23 E

Part 4

24 C   25 A   26 B   27 C   28 A   29 C   30 B

Transcript   *This is the Cambridge First Certificate in English Listening Test. Test Three.*

I'm going to give you the instructions for this test. I'll introduce each part of the test and give you time to look at the questions. At the start of each piece you'll hear this sound:

tone

You'll hear each piece twice.

Remember, while you're listening, write your answers on the question paper. You'll have five minutes at the end of the test to copy your answers onto the separate answer sheet.

There will now be a pause. Please ask any questions now, because you must not speak during the test.

[pause]

Now open your question paper and look at Part One.

[pause]

PART 1   *You'll hear people talking in eight different situations. For questions 1 to 8, choose the best answer, A, B or C.*

Question 1   *One.*
You overhear a man talking about an experience he had at an airport.
What did he lose?
A his passport
B his wallet
C a piece of luggage

[pause]

tone

The airport staff looked everwhere for it. It was terrible. I thought the plane was going to go without me. At first I thought someone must have taken it. Although my money wasn't inside, I'd bought some nice presents for the family. Then I remembered that I'd been to the washroom and I must have put it down in there. Luckily, I had my documents and boarding card in my jacket pocket and, to cut a long story short, I had to get on the plane without it. The airport staff sent it on to me three days later.

[pause]

tone

[The recording is repeated.]

[pause]

Question 2   *Two.*
You hear an advertisement on the radio.
What is special about the Fretlight guitar?
A It plays recorded music.
B It teaches you how to play.
C It plugs into a computer.

[pause]

tone

The *Fretlight* is a fully functional guitar that comes in acoustic and electric models. Built into its body is an on-board computer and a hundred and thirty-two lights that show you where to put your fingers. Simply flip a switch and choose the chord or note that you would like to play, and the finger positions for making the appropriate notes will be promptly displayed on the neck of the guitar. Beginners can get a real feel for the fingerboard, while the more experienced players will be able to discover lots of new musical possibilities …

[pause]

tone

[The recording is repeated.]

[pause]

Question 3 | *Three.*
You hear part of a radio programme.
What is the presenter talking about?
A food safety
B meal times
C healthy recipes

[pause]

tone

Whether you have just one large meal a day, or a number of small meals, there are some basic steps to keep you in good health. Ideally, eat food as soon as it is cooked or prepared. If you are preparing food for later use, keep cold foods in the fridge and hot foods hot until they are ready to be eaten. Piping hot, that's how cooked food should be, especially when it's reheated. And remember, prepared foods left at room temperature will not keep long, however fresh the ingredients you have used.

[pause]

tone

[The recording is repeated.]

[pause]

Question 4 | *Four.*
You hear two people discussing a type of pollution.
What do the speakers agree about?
A the best way to solve the problem
B how they feel about this type of pollution
C how they reacted to the solution they saw

[pause]

tone

Woman: Do you know what they were doing in town the other day? I had to rush away because it set my teeth on edge, but they were chipping the chewing gum off the paths with sharp tools.

Man: You know, I only realised recently that all those black spots on the ground are actually old chewing gum.

Woman: I mean, it's disgusting, isn't it?

Man: Deeply.

Woman: And what a nasty job!

Man: Well, I was actually there when the city once tested out a machine for this and, I had to laugh, it needed such a powerful suck to get it off, it lifted the stones themselves.

[pause]

tone

[The recording is repeated.]

[pause]

Question 5
Five.
You hear a conversation between a shop assistant and a customer about a compact disc.
What was the cause of the problem?
A The customer gave the wrong number.
B A mistake was made on the order form.
C The disc was incorrectly labelled.

[pause]

tone

Shop assistant: And you ordered it two weeks ago? Well, I can't find anything in the order book ... Oh, yes, here it is. Well, it seems we chased it up after you phoned and they said they couldn't find the order, so we gave them the details again. It hasn't turned up though. Oh, perhaps ... here's a note on the order form. They then told us there's nothing under the number you gave us, I'm afraid.
Customer: Well, I noted it down very carefully. Look.
Shop assistant: Uh-huh. Oh, I see. Two figures are the wrong way round on our form, that's why they couldn't find the disc.

[pause]

tone

[The recording is repeated.]

[pause]

Question 6
Six.
You overhear a conversation at a football game.
What does the speaker say about his team?
A They're better than usual.
B They're as good as he expected.
C They tend to be unlucky.

[pause]

tone

Man 1:   Not many here today, are there?

Man 2:   I guess it isn't as popular as it used to be. A few years ago it was so crowded here, you were lucky if you could see over all the heads. This is the first time I've been this season. I was expecting to see them lose – as ever – but I can't wait for the second half if they carry on playing like this.

[pause]

tone

[The recording is repeated.]

[pause]

Question 7   *Seven.*
You overhear a schoolgirl talking to her friend.
What does she think about her new teacher?
A He is clever.
B He is funny.
C He is interesting.

[pause]

tone

It's funny, I've had loads of maths teachers and they all seemed to be the same – really clever with figures but useless at dealing with children. That's why I used to play about in lessons and do anything for a laugh. But Mr Jones is something else. He's quite serious and he makes us work really hard and gives us loads of problems to solve, but what I like is he relates everything to real life.

[pause]

tone

[The recording is repeated.]

[pause]

Question 8   *Eight.*
In a hotel you overhear a conversation.
Who is the woman?
A a tour guide
B a tourist
C a hotel receptionist

[pause]

tone

Man: Oh, by the way, what's this all-island trip like then?

Woman: It lasts all day and you get picked up from the hotel at about seven thirty and they take you around the island to look at the sights.

Man:	Do you think it's worth going on then?
Woman:	I'd say so. You see all the sights and have lunch in a restaurant by the sea. The price includes everything, you know, like the museum and everything. The whole family enjoyed it when we went.

[pause]

tone

[The recording is repeated.]

[pause]

That's the end of Part One.

Now turn to Part Two.

[pause]

PART 2   *You'll hear part of a radio interview with a swimming instructor. For questions 9 to 18, complete the sentences.*

You now have forty-five seconds in which to look at Part Two.

[pause]

tone

Interviewer:	And now for our sports section, and I have with me today Paul Collison who is a swimming instructor with a rather unusual approach. Thanks for taking the time during your holiday to come and talk to us, Paul.
Paul:	It's very kind of you to invite me.
Interviewer:	Paul – you're *the* swimming instructor at the Palace Hotel in the south of France. How long have you been there?
Paul:	Oh, well I started working there in 1970 when I was eighteen years old.
Interviewer:	And you've never moved?
Paul:	Nope – I get to meet a lot of famous people there and … I guess I enjoy that.
Interviewer:	And of course a lot of them go there because they want *you* to teach them to swim!
Paul:	That's true, but I teach plenty of other people too – and not all my students are beginners.
Interviewer:	But we're not talking about young children, are we?
Paul:	Not usually – there isn't the same challenge teaching children. They have an almost natural ability to swim. Adults are afraid, and helping them overcome that is hard but much more fun somehow.
Interviewer:	But don't a lot of people just give up trying to learn once they reach a certain age?
Paul:	Not at all. I get hundreds of calls from people looking for 'sympathetic' instructors. I would estimate that about fifty per cent of the adult population can't swim – but they're still keen to learn.
Interviewer:	So it's just fear that holds them back?
Paul:	Basically, yes. I come across it all the time and it isn't just beginners. I have students who can swim a bit, but don't make any progress because – like all of them – they hate going *under* water.

Interviewer:	Mmm … So what's the secret, Paul?
Paul:	Well, you've got to relax in the water and that means that you *must* control your breathing.
Interviewer:	And I understand you have a special technique to help people do that.
Paul:	Yes, before my students even go into the pool I teach them how to breathe and to do that I give everyone a salad bowl.
Interviewer:	A salad bowl? Right …
Paul:	Everyone in the group gets one of these … each full of water. First, I get them to breathe … slowly through the nose and mouth … just normal controlled breathing.
Interviewer:	To calm them.
Paul:	Uh-huh … and then – they all have to put their faces in the bowl and breathe out under water.
Interviewer:	How does it go?
Paul:	Well, they're all terrified at first. So we repeat the exercise many times and in the end they become quite competitive about who can keep their face down the longest!
Interviewer:	And that means they've started to forget about their fear.
Paul:	Exactly. When I'm sure they're more confident about breathing, I move the group into the pool and I tell them that they are going to begin by trying to float with their faces in the water. Once I'm sure they're OK, I start them off and I teach different swimming strokes to different pupils depending on which one I think they'll find easiest. The swimming technique itself is far less important than feeling confident in the water.
Interviewer:	Great. So how many lessons would I need to learn to swim?
Paul:	Well, all my lessons are an hour long and generally it just takes three to overcome the fear and get people swimming. A few never make it but I'd say ninety per cent end up swimmers.
Interviewer:	So there's hope for us all yet … and now on to …

[pause]

Now you'll hear Part Two again.

tone

[The recording is repeated.]

[pause]

That's the end of Part Two.

Now turn to Part Three.

[pause]

PART 3   *You'll hear part of a radio programme called 'Morning Market'. Five listeners have telephoned the programme because they have something to sell. For questions 19 to 23, choose which of the statements, A to F, matches the reason each of the people gives for selling their possession. Use the letters only once. There is one extra letter which you do not need to use.*

You now have thirty seconds in which to look at Part Three.

[pause]

tone

Speaker One

[pause]

I've got a brand-new rowing machine. I won it actually, about two months ago, and it's still in its box. It's got an electric timer on it which tells you how much rowing you've done and all that. So anyone who's into exercise can do lots of rowing and keep fit and healthy. It folds up really small, so, you know, it won't take up too much space in, like, a bedroom or anything. I mean, I'll never use it because I was after the holiday which was won by whoever came first in the competition. So I'm looking for around forty-five pounds and my number is …

[pause]

Speaker Two

[pause]

I've got a kidney-shaped bath, colour soft cream, for sale. It's still in its original packing case because I ordered the wrong colour, you know, it didn't go with the rest of the bathroom suite I'd got. So, I contacted, you know, the suppliers who said they'll send me a replacement, at a price, of course! But I've now got to get rid of this one. It cost originally a hundred and seventy-five pounds and I'm letting it go for fifty if anyone's interested. OK? My number's …

[pause]

Speaker Three

[pause]

I've got a real bargain. It's a Lieberstein electric organ and it's got two keyboards and a rhythm section. It's in good condition, plays quite well, and it's not difficult to use or anything. But, what with us having a baby on the way, it's got to make way for more essential items, as we've only got a tiny flat at the moment. So, as I say, if anyone wants it, they can make me an offer. The only problem is, anyone interested would have to come and collect it. The number to ring is …

[pause]

Speaker Four

[pause]

Hello. I've got a lady's cycle for sale. I've got back trouble and I've been advised not to ride it, so rather than be tempted, I'll get rid of it. I hate the idea, because we're not well served with public transport out here and I used it quite a lot, but as I daren't ride it any more, I think it would be a mistake to hang on to it, you know, in case I had second thoughts. So, it's a Raleigh Chopper, pink, and I'd like thirty-five pounds for it, please. I can be contacted on …

[pause]

Speaker Five

[pause]

I've got two frying pans, you know, the sort for cooking stir-fry in, and a seven-piece tool set to go with them. All boxed and everything. Anyway, they've hardly been used because at one time I was intending to do a lot of this type of cooking because I've only got a small kitchenette, like, no oven. But I've been given a microwave instead now, so much easier to use. So, that's ten pounds for both pans and the tools and my number is …

[pause]

Now you'll hear Part Three again.

tone

[The recording is repeated.]

[pause]

That is the end of Part Three.

Now turn to Part Four.

[pause]

PART 4   *You'll hear an interview with a man who makes models for films and television. For questions 24 to 30, choose the best answer, A, B or C.*

You now have one minute in which to look at Part Four.

[pause]

tone

Interviewer: Matt Ryan makes models. He's worked for television and various other companies for many years. I went to his studio in London to talk to him. Matt, could I ask you to tell listeners a bit about your background and your early career?

Matt:	Sure. Well it's strange really, 'cos at first I never thought about model-making as a career. Fairly early on in my life I worked for a television channel … I really wanted a full-time job there, but the best I could get was holiday relief work, filling in for people while they were away. I started off in the photograph library and we had to collect pictures for the news, and it was a good way of getting into the business.
Interviewer:	So how did the career come about?
Matt:	I think it was an interesting time altogether really. It was the sixties and everyone was talking about going to the moon. There were comic books about space and models of astronauts. Where I was working we had photographs which were used in television reports on the subject. The scenes fascinated me and I thought why not build some three-dimensional kits or models of the views instead of these flat photos that were mostly black and white.
Interviewer:	And what happened to them?
Matt:	Something quite incredible really. I still think back on it with a lot of pride. During one of the space trips to the moon, the camera on the spacecraft burnt out and we had no pictures back in the television studio to put on the news. So they used a total of fifteen of my models as a substitute and they were broadcast to everyone at home.
Interviewer:	Do you think that marked the beginning of a career with television?
Matt:	Yes, because shortly after that, I was asked to go to a meeting with one of the TV heads. It was a time when they were looking for more people and I think nowadays that type of thing wouldn't happen – you'd need two degrees and about six years' experience! But they put me straight onto one of the biggest TV series at the time.
Interviewer:	What was that?
Matt:	It was called *Bright Star* and it was a children's programme they produced about a time traveller. You know the kind of thing … each week he had a different adventure in the twenty-first century and each time there would be monsters or strange creatures that he'd have to deal with, and I made most of the models for these. And I was just one of a whole load of people … you'd need make-up artists and scene-makers and costume designers … it was incredible.
Interviewer:	Can we move on to some other programmes that you've worked on because they haven't all been science fiction, have they?
Matt:	No. In fact the afternoon children's programmes were very demanding too. I made a regular appearance on these where I might talk about how to make your own toys or create your own set for a story, or run a competition based on space research.
Interviewer:	And you were also involved in documentaries at the time, weren't you?
Matt:	Yes … to be honest I did so many of them that I've lost count but my favourite was *Heart of Darkness* for which I won television prizes. That was quite funny because at the time it wasn't possible to get an award for what I did … you know, you could be best actor or best director but there was no category for special effects – well, only in films, not television – so they put my name forward for a lot of other things and I actually won seven of them!
Interviewer:	Matt, thank you for a fascinating interview.

[pause]

Now you'll hear Part Four again.

tone

[The recording is repeated.]

[pause]

That's the end of Part Four.

There'll now be a pause of five minutes for you to copy your answers onto the separate answer sheet. Be sure to follow the numbering of all the questions. I'll remind you when there is one minute left, so that you are sure to finish in time.

[Teacher, pause the recording here for five minutes. Remind your students when they have one minute left.]

That's the end of the test. Please stop now. Your supervisor will now collect all the question papers and answer sheets.

Test 4 Key

Paper 1   Reading (1 hour)

Part 1

1 B   2 C   3 A   4 D   5 A   6 B   7 C   8 C

Part 2

9 B   10 C   11 E   12 H   13 D   14 F   15 A

Part 3

16 B   17 C   18 D   19 B   20 A   21 E   22 A   23 C   24 A
25 D   26 C   27 B   28 E   29 D   30 E

Paper 2   Writing (1 hour 20 minutes)

Task-specific Mark Schemes

Part 1

Question 1

Content
The letter must include all the points in the notes:
1) respond enthusiastically to idea of holiday
2) state preference for month and explain why
3) state preference for event
4) suggest alternative topic.

Organisation and cohesion
Clear organisation of ideas, with suitable paragraphing and linking, and opening/closing formulae as appropriate to the task.

Appropriacy of register and format
Consistent register appropriate to the situation and target reader.

Range
Language relating to the functions above.
Vocabulary relating to travel and visit.

Target reader
Would be informed.

Part 2

Question 2

Content
Essay could agree or disagree with the statement, or discuss both sides of the argument.

Organisation and cohesion
Clear organisation of ideas, with suitable paragraphing and linking.

Appropriacy of register and format
Consistent register suitable to the situation and target reader.

Range
Language of describing, explaining and giving opinion.
Vocabulary relating to lifestyle of famous people.

Target reader
Would be informed.

Question 3

Content
Article should give information about people's homes in the future.

Organisation and cohesion
Clear organisation of ideas, with suitable paragraphing and linking.

Appropriacy of register and format
Consistent register suitable to the situation and target reader.

Range
Language of description and explanation.
Vocabulary relating to houses and homes.

Target reader
Would be informed.

Question 4

Content
Story should continue from prompt sentence.

Organisation and cohesion
Storyline should be clear. Paragraphing could be minimal. Should reach a definite ending, even if it is somewhat open-ended.

Appropriacy of register and format
Consistent register suitable to the story.

Range
Narrative tenses. Vocabulary appropriate to the chosen topic of story.

Target reader
Would be able to follow the storyline.

Question 5(a)

Content
Essay should explain how Julie's life changes after her husband's death.

Organisation and cohesion
Clear organisation of ideas, with suitable paragraphing and linking.

Appropriacy of register and format
Consistent register suitable to the situation and target reader.

Range
Language of description and explanation.
Vocabulary relating to story and plot.

Target reader
Would be informed.

Question 5(b)

Content
Letter should give writer's opinion of why *Pride and Prejudice* is still popular with people today.

Organisation and cohesion
Clear organisation of ideas, with suitable paragraphing and linking.

Appropriacy of register and format
Consistent register suitable to the situation and target reader.

Range
Language of description, explanation and opinion.
Vocabulary relating to story.

Target reader
Would be informed.

Paper 3 Use of English (45 minutes)

Part 1

1 D   2 C   3 D   4 B   5 C   6 C   7 D   8 A   9 B   10 C
11 D   12 A

Part 2

13 long   14 with   15 of   16 later/on   17 in   18 had/needed/used
19 to/for/before   20 takes   21 These   22 much   23 which   24 one

Part 3

25 extraordinary   26 freezing/frozen   27 assistance   28 equipment
29 loneliness   30 hopeful   31 friendships   32 heat   33 poisonous
34 reasonable

Part 4

35 never seen | such a **strange**   36 were **driven** | into town by   37 **insisted** on | paying
38 didn't **succeed** | in persuading   39 you **mind** | not using   40 made a **good** |
impression on   41 **wishes** (that) he had | told   42 had **trouble** | (in) following

Paper 4   Listening (approximately 40 minutes)

Part 1

1 A   2 A   3 B   4 A   5 C   6 A   7 C   8 C

Part 2

9 circle (around them)   10 (a) brain(s)   11 stress   12 feelings   13 read
14 reward   15 52 teeth   16 two days   17 sound wave(s)/sound(s) / high-pitched
noises   18 (fishing) nets

Part 3

19 E   20 F   21 C   22 D   23 B

Part 4

24 A   25 C   26 B   27 A   28 A   29 C   30 B

Transcript   *This is the Cambridge First Certificate in English Listening Test. Test Four.*

I'm going to give you the instructions for this test. I'll introduce each part of the test and give you time to look at the questions. At the start of each piece you'll hear this sound:

tone

You'll hear each piece twice.

Remember, while you're listening, write your answers on the question paper. You'll have five minutes at the end of the test to copy your answers onto the separate answer sheet.

There will now be a pause. Please ask any questions now, because you must not speak during the test.

[pause]

Now open your question paper and look at Part One.

[pause]

PART 1   *You'll hear people talking in eight different situations. For questions 1 to 8, choose the best answer, A, B or C.*

Question 1   One.
You overhear some people talking at a party in a hotel.
Where did the people first meet each other?
A at school
B at work
C at a wedding

[pause]

tone

Man:	Is Mark Hobson here?
Woman:	He's got a crisis at work and couldn't come. But Julie's here somewhere. Did you know he married Julie? You know, the girl who could never spell anything!
Man:	Oh, right.
Woman:	It's their wedding anniversary today, actually. She says she'd rather be here with her childhood friends than waiting at home for Mark to finish work!
Man:	Has he changed much?
Woman:	Well, he looks much the same as he did all those years ago.

[pause]

tone

[The recording is repeated.]

[pause]

Question 2   Two.
You overhear a conversation in a restaurant.
Why haven't they seen each other lately?
A He has been too busy.
B He has been ill.
C He has been away.

[pause]

tone

Man:	Hello, Jean!
Woman:	Mike Carstairs! My favourite customer. You haven't been in for ages.

Man:	No, I haven't, that's right.
Woman:	How are you?
Man:	I'm fine. I heard you weren't well.
Woman:	Well, I was away for a couple of weeks. But I'm fine now. Ah! You were going to the States, weren't you?
Man:	That fell through.
Woman:	Oh, did it?
Man:	What I've been doing is reorganising the whole department non-stop since I saw you. Just haven't had a moment to myself. This is the first time I've been in here since Christmas.
Woman:	Well, it's good to see you. Are you ready to order?

[pause]

tone

[The recording is repeated.]

[pause]

Question 3   *Three.*
You overhear someone talking about a concert.
How did she feel at the time?
A angry
B frightened
C disappointed

[pause]

tone

It was really awful and I'd been so looking forward to it. Don't get me wrong, the music was brilliant and the show itself was really well done, but I'm sure they let too many people in – it was ever so crowded. I was right at the front and everyone was pushing me against the stage. I couldn't breathe and I was so scared I thought I was going to faint.

[pause]

tone

[The recording is repeated.]

[pause]

Question 4   *Four.*
You hear a writer of children's stories talking about books and compact discs.
What advantage does he think books have over compact discs?
A They may last for a longer time.
B They are easier to look after.
C They contain better quality material.

[pause]

tone

I was brought up with a respect for books, you know, always having clean hands, not bending the pages down, etc. and I certainly try to make sure mine are as well made as possible. I like to pick them up by the wrong bit and throw them around and so on, you know, to make sure they are strong. I think it's the permanence of books that sets them apart from the other media, don't you? Of course, what's more important is that you have good literature and good images and, I suppose, whether that's actually on a compact disc or in a book doesn't matter.

[pause]

tone

[The recording is repeated.]

[pause]

Question 5

Five.
You hear a husband and wife talking about their summer holidays.
What problem do they have?
A They really hate flying anywhere.
B They can never think of anywhere to go.
C They never agree about what to do.

[pause]

tone

Husband: You see, right from the time we first met it was obvious that Natalie and I wanted a particular kind of holiday – the trouble was, it wasn't the same! I like going off and doing my own thing. You know, history and museums – that's what interests me.

Wife: Well, I love markets and looking for bargains – so we end up sort of hating each other for two weeks or so, instead of having a really nice time together. The odd thing is that we see eye to eye all the rest of the time. It's just when we step on that plane – then the trouble starts!

[pause]

tone

[The recording is repeated.]

[pause]

Question 6	Six.
	You hear a researcher being asked about her work.
	What is she doing when she speaks?
	A denying an accusation
	B disproving a theory
	C accepting a criticism

[pause]

tone

Interviewer:	Now it's a bit suspicious that this research about glasses has been paid for by a contact lens company, isn't it? Is it genuine or are you having us on?
Researcher:	Not at all. We asked about a thousand people, most of whom wore glasses, some of whom didn't, and really asked them what they thought of glasses. Their responses were interesting, but didn't come from us; it's what they told us answering open-ended questions. And most of them said, while they thought that glasses could be, you know, pretty trendy and that some of them looked quite cool, that they didn't much like them.

[pause]

tone

[The recording is repeated.]

[pause]

Question 7	Seven.
	You overhear a woman talking to a friend on a train.
	What does the woman think of the course she has attended?
	A It has made her feel more confident.
	B It has made her feel less confident.
	C It hasn't made much difference to how she feels.

[pause]

tone

Well, the whole point was to build confidence and I'm sure most feel it succeeded, even if only partly. I must say I found it all very enjoyable, although I can't say I've benefited greatly. There was plenty of opportunity to get to know other people in the business, though, if you wanted to – you know the sort of thing, trips to restaurants and the theatre in the evenings.

[pause]

tone

[The recording is repeated.]

[pause]

Question 8   *Eight.*
You overhear a woman speaking on the radio.
What is she doing?
A complaining about something
B apologising for something
C explaining something

[pause]

tone

Man: So, shall we move on to the next subject?

Woman: I'm sorry, but I do think it's necessary to go through this again for the benefit of your listeners. Look, this is a crucial point and I don't think it can be stressed enough. As I was saying, the first thing that anyone with a complaint about their pension should do is put it in writing.

[pause]

tone

[The recording is repeated.]

[pause]

That's the end of Part One.

Now turn to Part Two.

[pause]

PART 2   *You'll hear a radio report about dolphins. For questions 9 to 18, complete the sentences.*

You now have forty-five seconds in which to look at Part Two.

[pause]

tone

Newsreader: And for our last news item today, a special report from Diane Hassan on an animal that is rapidly becoming known as 'man's best friend', the dolphin.

Diane: Last week, a twenty-eight-year-old diver who went swimming in the Red Sea with a group of dolphins learnt the hard way just how caring these creatures can be. When the diver was suddenly attacked by a shark, they saved him by forming a circle around him and frightening the shark away.

It's not the first time such a rescue has happened and it's been known for some time that dolphins will do for humans what they do for their own kind. They are, in fact, the only animals in the world whose brains match ours in terms of size, and their intelligence and ability to feel emotion continue to fascinate scientists and doctors alike. For some time now, their healing powers have been well known. A swim with a group of dolphins, for example, is a recognised 'medical' activity for everyday problems such as stress. But some dolphins are playing a far more serious medical role for us than that.

Amanda Morton, who suffered from a life-threatening illness, argued that being with dolphins *saved* her life because they were able to read her feelings. 'They knew how I was feeling,' she was quoted as saying. And it's the idea that they actually 'care', that they are gentle, happy creatures that want to befriend us, which has led to projects with children as well. In one such project, dolphins are being used to help children who are slow learners learn to read. The dolphins do things like carrying small boards on their noses. These boards show words or pictures which the children are asked to identify. When the children get it right, they spend more time swimming with the dolphins and touching them and they see this as a reward. So what is it that makes contact with dolphins so powerful? They certainly have an engaging smile … in each jaw they have up to fifty-two teeth, but rather than frightening us to death, it's one of the warmest greetings in the world! They're also fantastic swimmers to watch … the spotted dolphin has been observed reaching twenty miles an hour and keeping this up for two days at a time. And they *know* they're good at it so they show off in front of humans by diving in and out of the water and showing us just how much fun they're having. They're great communicators too. They make all kinds of fascinating high-pitched noises. They catch fish, for example, by sending out sound waves which tell them everything they need to know – where it is, what it is and how big it is.

   The only creatures that concern dolphins, in fact, are sharks and *man*. We don't necessarily harm them on purpose, but we trap them in fishing nets and we pollute the water they swim in. Pollution, in fact, is one of the dolphin's greatest problems. So with all the good they do for us, isn't it time we started caring about them?

[pause]

Now you'll hear Part Two again.

tone

[The recording is repeated.]

[pause]

That's the end of Part Two.

Now turn to Part Three.

[pause]

PART 3   *You'll hear five different people talking about the head teacher or principal of their former secondary school. For questions 19 to 23, choose from the list, A to F, what each speaker is saying. Use the letters only once. There's one extra letter which you do not need to use.*

You now have thirty seconds in which to look at Part Three.

[pause]

tone

Speaker One

[pause]

It's strange looking back because at the time you don't always appreciate people and certainly I think that's true of your teachers and particularly a head teacher. I mean she was always encouraging us not to drop litter and to think about things like preserving the countryside and so on, and she'd say, 'Don't you want your children to live in a better world?' But when you're fifteen, you can't imagine having a family – all you care about is getting your homework done and going out with your friends!

[pause]

Speaker Two

[pause]

I don't know if it's the same in all countries, but where I live your head teacher usually teaches classes too and we had our head for athletics. In one way it was exciting 'cos she was very good at it herself, like she could out-run any of the boys in our class, but whatever we were doing she was always pushing us to do it faster than anyone else or jump higher than our friends regardless of the talent or ability we had – and with some it was pointless.

[pause]

Speaker Three

[pause]

I think if it hadn't been for our head teacher, I'd be doing something quite different now. She used to assess our Art exams and although there were people in my class who were really talented artists … you know, they could paint anything from real life and it looked brilliant … she always preferred the more unusual stuff – she said it showed we had ideas of our own, and she really liked that, so, I did well. I mean, now I make a living putting designs on greeting cards.

[pause]

Speaker Four

[pause]

I always felt that our head teacher was under-valued and that she might have done better in a different environment … her own staff held her up a bit. They all seemed … oh, I don't know … maybe they just didn't like the idea of change … but I remember she wanted to introduce a new teaching method for French classes and the department head just dismissed the idea … and so many ideas she had which were never taken up are being used in schools today. I sometimes wonder how she feels.

[pause]

Speaker Five

[pause]

I've got some friends who say they left school and they suddenly felt lost. They'd spent a long time 'getting an education' but didn't know what to do once they'd got it. I think we were lucky because our head teacher built up a good network of contacts with local people and so they didn't mind giving us an insight into what it might be like, say, working in a hospital or office. I know it wasn't a new idea or anything but I think she gave us a good sense of direction which I've valued all my life.

[pause]

Now you'll hear Part Three again.

tone

[The recording is repeated.]

[pause]

That's the end of Part Three.

Now turn to Part Four.

[pause]

PART 4   *You will hear an interview with a tour leader who works for an adventure company in Africa. For questions 24 to 30, choose the best answer, A, B or C.*

You now have one minute in which to look at Part Four.

[pause]

tone

Announcer: And now for The Holiday Programme with Mandy Rice.
Mandy: Today I'm talking to Don Nicholson, a tour leader who spends ten months of the year looking after groups of up to eighteen tourists in southern Africa. They travel together in the back of a truck, put up their own tents and cook their own food. Welcome to the programme, Don.
Don: Thanks.
Mandy: This is a holiday with a difference, isn't it? Tell us, first of all, what sort of people go on a camping trip in Africa … and a long one at that … it is a month each trip?
Don: Yes. Well it sounds a sort of studenty thing to do, but in fact the majority of our passengers are people like doctors and lawyers. We do get some students but they tend to be the ones that are studying something like conservation or wildlife.

Mandy: And when do they all first meet?

Don: The evening before we set off. They fly in and I pick them up from the airport and immediately before we start sorting out places in the truck we go through what they've brought with them. Amazingly, every now and then we get somebody who genuinely doesn't realise it's a camping tour, so I have to rush out and get them blankets and a sleeping bag.

Mandy: It must be difficult – a whole group of strangers coming together and then having to live together like that.

Don: Mmm. It goes surprisingly well, but I always think the first day is critical because it sets the tone for the whole trip. We've had the odd nightmare start where we've got a flat tyre twenty minutes after we set off or it's dark and pouring with rain and people just can't get their tents up. Yeah, once we were making pasta late at night and the cook put in a tin of strawberry jam instead of tomato paste – those are the bad starts!

Mandy: Basically everyone has to take part in the domestic chores, do they?

Don: Yes. The brochure makes it clear that people have to work on a rota system and they usually do about an hour's work a day. We get a few who don't want to muck in but more often they are just untidy and I've got a bit of an eye for that because … well, they might leave a fork lying on the ground, for example, and okay, it's just a fork, but in a lot of places in Africa you can't get forks, so I'm quite possessive about the equipment.

Mandy: And do people really get on?

Don: A lot of people have never lived in a tight community situation like this before and you do get conflicts and personality clashes. The best approach is to observe it from afar. If it gets out of hand, I might point out in front of the whole group that there's a problem between certain people.

Mandy: Shame them a bit … .

Don: Mmm. Sometimes it works. To be fair, conflicts are rare but small problems *can* mount up in that kind of environment. Evening noise, for example. Some people want to go to sleep early and others don't. On occasions I've had to be the sort of go-between and impose a 'lights out' time if things start getting out of hand.

Mandy: What about getting up, because that's something we're really not keen on on holiday?

Don: If we're going into a wildlife park we might have to be on the road by six a.m. but people still ask why they have to get up so early. I've learnt how to do it now. If they're a quick group I'll get them up at five, but if they're slow I won't shout and scream at them – I just get them up at four thirty.

Mandy: Well, perhaps now we should go on to talk about what there is to see in some of those game parks that you have to get up so early for.

[pause]

Now you'll hear Part Four again.

tone

[The recording is repeated.]

[pause]

That's the end of Part Four.

There'll now be a pause of five minutes for you to copy your answers onto the separate answer sheet. Be sure to follow the numbering of all the questions. I'll remind you when there is one minute left, so that you're sure to finish in time.

[Teacher, pause the recording here for five minutes. Remind your students when they have one minute left.]

That's the end of the test. Please stop now. Your supervisor will now collect all the question papers and answer sheets.

Sample answer sheet: Paper 1

ESOL Examinations

S A M P L E

Candidate Name
If not already printed, write name
in CAPITALS and complete the
Candidate No. grid (in pencil).

Candidate Signature

Examination Title

Centre

Supervisor:
If the candidate is ABSENT or has WITHDRAWN shade here ▭

Centre No.

Candidate No.

Examination Details

0	0	0	0
1	1	1	1
2	2	2	2
3	3	3	3
4	4	4	4
5	5	5	5
6	6	6	6
7	7	7	7
8	8	8	8
9	9	9	9

Candidate Answer Sheet

Instructions

Use a PENCIL (B or HB).

Mark ONE letter for each
question.

For example, if you think
B is the right answer to
the question, mark your
answer sheet like this:

| 0 | A | B | D E F G H |

Rub out any answer you
wish to change using an
eraser.

1	A B C D E F G H
2	A B C D E F G H
3	A B C D E F G H
4	A B C D E F G H
5	A B C D E F G H
6	A B C D E F G H
7	A B C D E F G H
8	A B C D E F G H
9	A B C D E F G H
10	A B C D E F G H
11	A B C D E F G H
12	A B C D E F G H
13	A B C D E F G H
14	A B C D E F G H
15	A B C D E F G H
16	A B C D E F G H
17	A B C D E F G H
18	A B C D E F G H
19	A B C D E F G H
20	A B C D E F G H

21	A B C D E F G H
22	A B C D E F G H
23	A B C D E F G H
24	A B C D E F G H
25	A B C D E F G H
26	A B C D E F G H
27	A B C D E F G H
28	A B C D E F G H
29	A B C D E F G H
30	A B C D E F G H
31	A B C D E F G H
32	A B C D E F G H
33	A B C D E F G H
34	A B C D E F G H
35	A B C D E F G H
36	A B C D E F G H
37	A B C D E F G H
38	A B C D E F G H
39	A B C D E F G H
40	A B C D E F G H

UNIVERSITY *of* CAMBRIDGE
ESOL Examinations

SAMPLE

Candidate Name
If not already printed, write name
in CAPITALS and complete the
Candidate No. grid (in pencil).

Candidate Signature

Examination Title

Centre

Supervisor:
If the candidate is ABSENT or has WITHDRAWN shade here ⊂▭⊃

Centre No.

Candidate No.

Examination Details

0	0	0	0
1	1	1	1
2	2	2	2
3	3	3	3
4	4	4	4
5	5	5	5
6	6	6	6
7	7	7	7
8	8	8	8
9	9	9	9

Candidate Answer Sheet

Instructions
Use a PENCIL (B or HB). Rub out any answer you wish to change using an eraser.

Part 1: Mark ONE letter for each question.

For example, if you think **B** is the right
answer to the question, mark your
answer sheet like this:

| 0 | A | B | C | D |

Parts 2, 3 and **4:** Write your answer clearly
in CAPITAL LETTERS.

For Parts 2 and 3 write one letter
in each box. For example:

| 0 | E X A M P L E |

Part 1

1	A	B	C	D
2	A	B	C	D
3	A	B	C	D
4	A	B	C	D
5	A	B	C	D
6	A	B	C	D
7	A	B	C	D
8	A	B	C	D
9	A	B	C	D
10	A	B	C	D
11	A	B	C	D
12	A	B	C	D

Part 2

Do not write
below here

13		13 1 0 u
14		14 1 0 u
15		15 1 0 u
16		16 1 0 u
17		17 1 0 u
18		18 1 0 u
19		19 1 0 u
20		20 1 0 u
21		21 1 0 u
22		22 1 0 u
23		23 1 0 u
24		24 1 0 u

Continues over ➡

Part 3

		Do not write below here
25		25 1 0 u
26		26 1 0 u
27		27 1 0 u
28		28 1 0 u
29		29 1 0 u
30		30 1 0 u
31		31 1 0 u
32		32 1 0 u
33		33 1 0 u
34		34 1 0 u

Part 4

		Do not write below here
35		35 2 1 0 u
36		36 2 1 0 u
37		37 2 1 0 u
38		38 2 1 0 u
39		39 2 1 0 u
40		40 2 1 0 u
41		41 2 1 0 u
42		42 2 1 0 u

UNIVERSITY *of* CAMBRIDGE
ESOL Examinations

S A M P L E

Candidate Name
If not already printed, write name
in CAPITALS and complete the
Candidate No. grid (in pencil).

Candidate Signature

Examination Title

Centre

   Supervisor:
   If the candidate is ABSENT or has WITHDRAWN shade here ⊐

Test version: A B C D E F J K L M N   Special arrangements: S H

Centre No.

Candidate No.

**Examination
Details**

0	0	0	0
1	1	1	1
2	2	2	2
3	3	3	3
4	4	4	4
5	5	5	5
6	6	6	6
7	7	7	7
8	8	8	8
9	9	9	9

Candidate Answer Sheet

Instructions

Use a PENCIL (B or HB).
Rub out any answer you wish to change using an eraser.

Parts 1, 3 and **4:**
Mark ONE letter for each question.

For example, if you think **B** is the
right answer to the question, mark
your answer sheet like this:

Part 2:
Write your answer clearly in CAPITAL LETTERS.

Write one letter or number in each box.
If the answer has more than one word, leave one
box empty between words.

For example:

Turn this sheet over to start.

© UCLES 2008   Photocopiable

Sample answer sheet: Paper 4

Part 1

	A	B	C
1			
2			
3			
4			
5			
6			
7			
8			

Part 2 (Remember to write in CAPITAL LETTERS or numbers)

		Do not write below here
9		9 1 0 u
10		10 1 0 u
11		11 1 0 u
12		12 1 0 u
13		13 1 0 u
14		14 1 0 u
15		15 1 0 u
16		16 1 0 u
17		17 1 0 u
18		18 1 0 u

Part 3

	A	B	C	D	E	F
19						
20						
21						
22						
23						

Part 4

	A	B	C
24			
25			
26			
27			
28			
29			
30			